House Beautiful

Your Dream Kitchen

Stylish Solutions for the Home

House Beautiful

Your
Dream Kitchen

Stylish Solutions for the Home

Liz George
and the editors of *House Beautiful*

HEARST BOOKS
A Division of Sterling Publishing Co., Inc.
NEW YORK

Produced by Spooky Cheetah Press, Stamford, CT
Written by Liz George
Edited by Brian Fitzgerald
Interior Design by Kimberly Shake
Cover Design by Margaret Rubiano

Library of Congress Cataloging-in-Publication Data
George, Liz.
    House beautiful your dream kitchen : stylish solutions
for the home /Liz George.
        p. cm.
    Includes index.
    ISBN 1-58816-425-X
        1. Kitchens—Design and construction. 2. Kitchens—
Remodeling. I. House beautiful. II. Title.
TX653.G46 2005
643'.3--dc22
                                        2005040248

10 9 8 7 6 5 4 3 2 1

Published by Hearst Books
A Division of Sterling Publishing Co., Inc.
387 Park Avenue South, New York, NY 10016

House Beautiful is a trademark owned by Hearst Magazines
Property, Inc., in USA, and Hearst Communications, Inc., in
Canada. Hearst Books is a trademark owned by Hearst
Communications, Inc.

www.housebeautiful.com

For information about custom editions, special sales,
premium and corporate purchases, please contact
Sterling Special Sales Department at 800-805-5489
or specialsales@sterlingpub.com.

Distributed in Canada by Sterling Publishing
c/o Canadian Manda Group, 165 Dufferin Street
Toronto, Ontario, Canada M6K 3H6

Distributed in Australia by Capricorn Link
(Australia) Pty. Ltd.
P.O. Box 704, Windsor, NSW 2756 Australia

Printed in China

ISBN 1-58816-425-X

contents

foreword

By opening this book, you've pledged to never utter the words "ordinary" and "kitchen" in the same sentence again. *Your Dream Kitchen* is about envisioning, planning and realizing a space that surpasses the everyday and embodies everything you hoped a kitchen could be...and then some.

There's truly no other room in the house that conjures up as many positive associations as the kitchen. From tempting aromas of memorable meals to sharing a soothing cup of tea, our kitchens feed both body and soul. They also play an important role in making anyone who enters our homes feel welcome. With that in mind, your dream kitchen has to be more than just functional and attractive.

Your Dream Kitchen helps you find that "something more" by taking you on a journey through the exciting phases of design and style with page after page of glorious, unique and well-planned kitchens of every style, size and configuration. We'll also guide you through the important elements that, when combined, create kitchens that are worth every penny—and second of time—spent.

With *Your Dream Kitchen* as your companion, you'll have the motivation, inspiration and—most important—the information you need to design a space that will live up to *your* dreams and bring your family joy for many years to come.

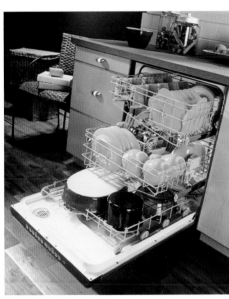

DESIGN & STYLE

◀ This well-planned kitchen is rich in details like a decorative tile mural and beautiful moldings.

kitchens by design

Designing a dream kitchen is a creative challenge that can be exciting, a little intimidating and, more often than not, all-consuming! But for anyone who loves to spend a lot of time in the kitchen, planning the ideal kitchen—a space where you can work, cook, eat and entertain at the same time—makes perfect sense.

Kitchens are no longer isolated workrooms in which the cook labors alone and cabinets and appliances serve only a utilitarian purpose. As kitchens take center stage in homes and continue to reign as the most important home-improvement space, expectations are a lot higher.

The elements that all well-conceived kitchens have in common are adequate space to prepare meals and gather friends and family, as well as a style that reflects the owner's unique needs and taste. Turning your kitchen dreams into a reality starts in the design stage. Everything from devising a kitchen layout that makes life easier to choosing colors and improving storage options are on these pages—including smart ideas to make your kitchen welcoming and accessible to everyone. By considering these expert design ideas, you can dramatically improve the raw kitchen space you have to work with and achieve that "perfect" kitchen you've already started to envision.

planning

▲ This congenial Southern-style kitchen generates a welcoming atmosphere. The work zones are shrewdly separated from social space by a well-placed peninsula.

Smart kitchen planning starts by taking a good long look at your space and considering it in regard to your needs and your wish list. A good design should not only be functional, it should be special in the sense that it suits both your lifestyle and aesthetic sensibilities.

Asking the right questions can help make planning easier. In the case of a remodel, considering what you want from your new kitchen—improved aesthetics, modern amenities, a more effi-cient layout or increased resale value for your home—can help focus your energies. If you plan to live in the house for some time, the years you will enjoy your kitchen can justify the expense of including certain high-end features.

Since today's kitchens often open to one or more other spaces, the room's overall look is more important than ever before. Considering your kitchen in relation to your entire home is an important first step in planning. Adding unique elements, such as archi-tectural glass, custom-designed hoods or tile murals, can't be afterthoughts. Likewise, if you eventually plan to add an addition, take care not to position plumbing or structural elements in spots that will obstruct future work.

Lack of space presents another plan-ning challenge, but it doesn't have to be a limitation. Cozy kitchens have their charm, and there are plenty of ways to create the illusion of more space and light. Choosing light-colored counter-tops and paint for the walls, opting for

Although compact in size, this well-conceived kitchen offers ample counter and display space. Light colors on the cabinets and open shelving also contribute to the room's airy feeling.

Create a Mood

Now is the time to plan for any little special touches you'll want to add to your new kitchen.

ADD INSTANT AMBIANCE: Most people plan their kitchen lighting to provide ample illumination for prep work and dining. But don't forget to consider lighting needs when your kitchen is off-duty. A dimmer can create a mellow mood after-hours; illumination above or under cabinets creates subtle evening lighting, perfect for midnight kitchen runs.

WORK TO YOUR OWN SOUNDTRACK: A good sound system can make light work of kitchen drudgery and drown out whirring blenders and clanking pans. Plan to wire your kitchen with speakers, ideally connected to your home's central audio system or a kitchen stereo, for the best sound possible.

A beautiful tile backsplash and vibrant oven knobs add to this kitchen's appeal.

If your kitchen can't accommodate an island, consider a chopping-block table.

glazed or shiny cabinets and installing ambient lighting are all ways to design a space that seems open and airy.

Be sure to keep cleanup in mind while you're planning your space. For example, glossy paint wipes up better than matte or semigloss; glass-topped tables show fingerprints; a smooth-top electric range has no messy burners to clean; and an integral sink has no seams to trap dirt.

A good atmosphere in your kitchen also depends on proper ventilation. A quality ventilation system, whether in the form of a range hood or downdraft system, can keep grease, odors and humidity from polluting your home.

By planning early, you also can allow the kitchen's range hood to become a focal point. Whether you choose sleek stainless, warm copper, dramatic glass or even rustic tile, making a definitive design statement with a range hood can help the rest of the room's style come together.

Layout

Most kitchen designs follow some version of the work triangle. With this setup, all key workstations, including the cooktop, refrigerator and sink, are connected in an imaginary triangle. In a perfect workspace, all three are within a pivot of one another, so no extra steps or turns are required during meal prep. An ideal kitchen has been described as one in which each "leg" of the triangle is between four and nine feet long. Total length of all three legs should equal between 12 and 26 feet and cabinetry should not intersect any triangle leg by more than 12 inches. Of course, general traffic patterns should not interfere with the triangle.

There are four common kitchen layouts based on the work triangle. These are the galley shape, L-shape, U-shape and G-shape. Familiarizing yourself with the features of each can help you determine which setup will work best in your space.

▼ Thanks to careful planning, this open-floor design creates separate zones for dining, cooking, working and relaxing that coexist in perfect harmony.

GALLEY SHAPE

Most often adopted in a small space, the galley kitchen consists of two facing walls of appliances and fixtures flanking a relatively narrow aisle. The close proximity of each element makes this a particularly efficient layout—for one cook.

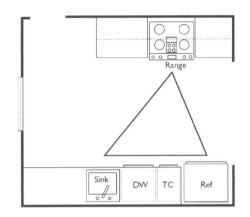

L-SHAPE

In the "L" configuration, the three main elements are located along two perpendicular walls, forming a natural work triangle. Depending on the size of the space, this configuration offers generous counter area and can include an island.

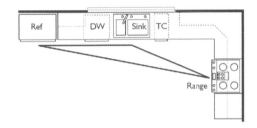

U-SHAPE

In this layout, the sink, range and refrigerator are arranged on three walls, affording the same efficiency as the galley with the potential for more elbow room. The "U" offers the potential for multiple work triangles: cooking, baking, even a butler's pantry. Also, instead of a wall, one arm of the "U" can be transformed into an informal dining area that opens into the next room, allowing guests to interact with the cook.

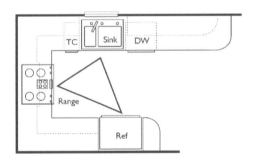

G-SHAPE

Essentially a U-shape layout with a fourth wall, this layout allows for more cabinetry, appliances or amenities than the other three layouts. The fourth wall may be a peninsula, a partial wall or a pass-through.

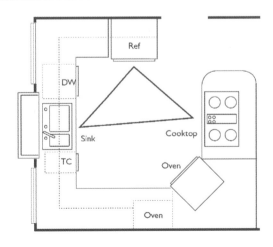

▲ Planning stages are a great time to consider different options, such as including a booth or bench-style seating in lieu of a traditional dining set.

Plan Something Special

Now is the time to consider alternatives to traditional design and ways you can tailor your kitchen to your needs. Rather than choosing one surface for counters, for example, consider combining surfaces, such as wood and stainless steel. This will bring excitement and added function to your kitchen while keeping costs down.

Cooking style also can affect how you plan your new kitchen layout. You can designate different areas for cooking, baking and roasting by eliminating the traditional range from your design plans and opting instead for a separate cooktop and double wall ovens.

If entertaining large groups is something you do frequently, a second sink and/or second dishwasher could allow you more time with guests. Cooking and chatting simultaneously can also be achieved by placing a stove in an island, allowing guests to gather 'round during dinner preparation.

Probably the most important thing to consider during planning is that you stay true to the "architectural bones" of your kitchen. There's nothing worse than taking a period home and ripping out the very kitchen details that make it unique. Better to maintain architectural integrity and integrate period details such as cabinets and dumbwait-

▲ A wine cooler built right into the kitchen island is the perfect addition for people who love to entertain.

ers with newer additions. In the end, your kitchen design will exude more personality and appeal as a result.

Plan to Work

No matter its size or shape, any kitchen can benefit from a well-designed niche dedicated to organizing household affairs. After all, the kitchen seems to be the place where the business of keeping the family going occurs. Creating a command post in this hub can keep things running smoothly. This planning desk can take many forms, depending on the principal user's work habits and the amount of available space. Minimum requirements include a surface to write on, seating, storage and access to a telephone.

Aesthetically, the planning desk should appear as part of the kitchen's overall scheme. A high-tech-looking workstation would be completely out of place in a country-style kitchen, for instance. Most important, the planning desk should be removed from the work triangle, as well as from the secondary prep area.

Four feet of counter space with one legal-sized file drawer and a pencil drawer is the average configuration for a planning desk, but you can get by with less and personalize the space to suit your needs. New design innovations include features like a roll-top akin to an appliance garage for stowing away a personal computer. You can add shelves, cubbyholes, even a corkboard to display your kids' school papers and artwork.

▲ An expanse of the kitchen counter has been lowered to 30-inch desk height to create an out-of-the-way workspace.

▲ A curved desktop creates space in a tight area. An adjacent cabinet stows supplies.

▲ Open cubbies for mail and address books make for a cozy and efficient work area.

Get in Touch with Color

Envision lemon yellow, Tuscan terracotta, celery green or merlot red. The color you respond to most can reveal a lot about what makes you feel comfortable. Selecting the right hue for a room is part art, part science. No matter how fashionable a color is, if it doesn't please you, it isn't the right choice. The most important aspect of choosing color is surrounding yourself with something that will be pleasing.

Once a base color is selected, that color plays an important role in determining the tone of a room. Cool colors, for instance—blues, greens and purples—have been proven to be soothing, while hot colors—reds, oranges and yellows—exhilarate and excite. The latter is often a choice for kitchens and dining areas as it can stimulate appetite. Again, if they are not your favorites, you should feel free to choose cooler hues. Beyond choosing a single base color is the importance of how color combinations will influence a space. No color appears in a vacuum, and the choice of combinations is vast. A base color can be augmented with varying values (lightness and darkness) or intensities (brightness and dullness) of the same color. Or you can choose to incorporate entirely new colors, either opposites or complementary colors.

Color Cues

Before settling on a color, experiment with several in the space. The most important thing is to choose colors that "feel" right to you. Cover as large a swath as possible with the candidates and view the colors at different times of day, in every type of lighting. Be sure to keep in mind that colors look more intense in large doses. Notice how colors are influenced by what surrounds them. For example, white cabinets topped with blue granite can make white walls look powder blue.

Familiarize yourself with the color wheel. Complementary colors—those located across the wheel from one another, such as red and green or yellow and purple—appear vibrant when combined. Analogous colors—those adjacent to one another, such as blue and green or yellow and orange—are more soothing combinations.

Choose one dominant color and two subordinates. Use the dominant color most and incorporate the other two in smaller doses, such as in a backsplash.

▼ Color is one of the first planning decisions for your kitchen. Often the color you choose ties in to the mood you want to create and complements the style of the kitchen.

Consider values. When pairing complementary colors, choose those with similar values. For instance, a strong red looks best with a strong (rather than a pale) yellow. When working with a single color, however, use varying values to create visual interest.

Find a happy medium. If you plan to use a dark and a light color in the same space, include a third to act as an intermediary between the two. In a room with black countertops and cream-colored cabinets, a warm caramel color, such as a wood table or a tumbled marble backsplash in this hue, can serve as a pleasing visual bridge between the two opposites.

▲ Stylish and fun, this retro refrigerator adds a dash of color and whimsy to any kitchen.

Take a Smile Test

If you're not sure which colors are right for your kitchen, try the "smile" test. Gather a variety of colors, textures and patterns, using fabric swatches, paint chips or wallpaper and flooring samples. Then see how you and your family respond to each one on an emotional level. Those samples and swatches that garner a smile are the ones that should make the cut. By taking this test, you'll find that your natural preferences will emerge with very little conscious effort from you.

smart design

Remodeling a kitchen is a huge investment of time and money—and it's one you don't want to make more than once! The best way to ensure your kitchen remains comfortable and functional for years to come is by incorporating the principles of universal design.

Originally conceived as a means of improving accessibility for the disabled and aged populations, universal design really does provide an overall improvement in kitchen usage. Countertops, appliances, shelving and storage are designed to provide convenient use for everyone in the house—whether they are tall or short, young or old or just hate needing a stepladder to access items on impossibly high shelves.

Popular universal design elements include varying the height of countertops to create a workspace for everyone, lowering above-counter cabinets so they're no higher than 48 inches from the floor and raising bottom cabinets six inches or so to reduce the need for bending. Placing pull-out shelves in low cabinets and installing draws that fully extend provides easier access to supplies. Another smart idea is replacing hard-to-handle cabinet knobs with easy-to-grasp handles, installing faucets with easy-grip lever handles and choosing slip-resistant flooring.

You should be sure to consider your appliances in terms of universal design, as well. That applies to the kind of features they offer and where they are located in your new kitchen design.

Opt for a smooth-surface cooktop and install it so that it is level with your counter—this allows the cook to slide heavy pots and pans rather than lift them. Placing your microwave at counter level rather than over the range allows older children to safely prepare a hot snack. Other ideas to consider include raising your dishwasher about eight inches off the floor. This will minimize the strain on your back and accommodate a wheelchair user.

By making simple adjustments like these, you can plan a kitchen that's comfortable for users of any size, age and ability, and that increases the value of your home at resale.

▲ This island includes a butler's sink that allows everyone to pitch in with meal prep.

STYLE NOTES

Universal Appeal
Simple modifications can make your kitchen welcoming for everyone. Lower light switches to 44 inches from the floor to afford access to a seated person or a child. For wheelchair accessibility, allow for a 32-inch-wide doorway.

▲ Including a smooth-surface cooktop on this island means there'll be less heavy lifting for the family chef.

▲ A separate small sink surrounded by butcher-block countertops is the perfect place for a helper to prepare produce.

Go High-Tech

When it comes to outfitting your kitchen, a.k.a. "command central," it's not uncommon to yearn for a few high-tech whistles and bells. After all, increasing the convenience factor of the space guarantees it will be a place you can enjoy for years to come. High-tech kitchen features have come a long way from speed cooking or dishwashers that run silently. Home-control and entertainment features are creating kitchens worthy of their reputations as a home's nerve center.

Beyond the addition of a TV in the kitchen, new kitchen designs are incorporating space-saving units that combine TV with the convenience of Internet access and DVD capability, so home chefs can watch movies while cooking Thanksgiving dinner or check e-mails over breakfast. Among the futuristic advances to look for when planning your new kitchen are microwaves with scanning wands to read and follow directions on food packages and connected home devices that are networked to save time and

money. In-ceiling speakers are decidedly high-tech, yet offer an aesthetically pleasing, almost invisible alternative to their traditional counterparts.

Play It Safe

Kitchens should be warm, welcoming and, of course, safe. During project planning, keep in mind that electrical sources are among the leading causes of house fires. All electrical outlets in kitchens should be on a ground-fault interrupter circuit. Label all circuit breakers by the area they serve and be

▼ Far from institutional, this kitchen features base cabinets that are raised to provide convenient access to wheelchair users—proving that universal design can be great looking, too.

sure your home offers adequate power and sufficient outlets to run all appliances. Use safe cover plates on all switches and outlets and, if small children live in the home, install child-safe outlet covers.

The best way to make kitchen cabinets off-limits to small children is to install inexpensive, childproof latches. For extra protection, designate a high cabinet to store dangerous cleansers and chemicals. Choose a range or cooktop with lockout features and select an edging on countertops that's rounded. Plan adequate storage for small appliances, so neither appliances nor cords are within reach of curious little hands.

▲ Locating the dishwasher off the floor means less bending and stooping for you. Placing a drawer underneath provides a great spot for storing items not frequently needed.

▲ Gas ranges with a lockout function on the console can prevent children from accidentally turning on burners.

The Ultimate Fridge

This Internet refrigerator features an ice maker and water tap built into its front casing, as well as a built-in 15-inch TV with web-surfing capabilities, a stereo and a digital camera. The monitor screen is detachable for easy cleaning. And if that weren't enough, the refrigerator can help with shopping, too. An automated inventory feature can tell you what's inside without opening the door, inform you how long it's been since your last grocery run and warn you when you run low on your favorite foods. You can even access most of the unit's features remotely, via the Internet or a web-enabled cell phone or PDA. And how's this for high-tech? The fridge's calendar will remind you of special events.

storage

▲ Clever storage techniques help this kitchen retain its good looks. An appliance garage and microwave cubby help keep countertops uncluttered. A stainless-steel rack for measuring cups keeps the utensils at hand while also adding an interesting design touch.

No other room benefits more from the notion of "a place for everything and everything in its place" than the kitchen. Yet in between considering work triangles and the latest gadgets, storage needs might seem overly simplistic. Even if you assume your renovation plan already affords you more storage than you currently have, spending time to design specific storage spaces that best suit various tools, small appliances, utensils and pantry items can bring order to chaos.

There's something incredibly soothing and stimulating about walking into a kitchen where clutter is at a minimum. Organizing cabinets and drawers ensures all the necessary tools can be found without a hunt or a struggle. Without the distractions of pots and pans, gadgets and other paraphernalia, the kitchen becomes an inviting space that encourages lingering.

Planning ahead for storage requires taking stock of what you have. Do you want appliances concealed in cabinets

Discover Drawer Power

Deep base cabinets require bending to extract items; roll-out shelves require you to open cabinet doors to access shelves. But drawers trump all these cabinet systems by requiring nothing more than a single pulling motion to access what you need. If you replace some of your kitchen cabinets with drawers, include at least two deep drawers for pots and pans and a bank of shallow drawers for utensils, linens, even spices.

▲ Dividers that partition drawers into separate compartments prevent large drawers from turning into junk drawers.

▲ Swing-out shelves, available in a variety of depths, enable you to get the most out of corner cabinets.

▲ This pull-down drawer keeps cleanup tools at the ready—without taking away from the look of the cabinetry.

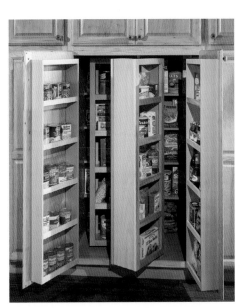

▲ When there's no space for a walk-in pantry, a system of swing-out shelves can offer the same amount of storage in a compact space.

where they can be accessed easily? Do you need drawers for linens or shelves for cookbooks? Most people say they can't have too much kitchen storage space, which is why pantries are more important than ever. Options abound, from armoires with pull-out shelves to cabinets with movable baskets. If your kitchen designer or cabinetmaker has limited choices, check with a closet expert who specializes in pantries. Then plan to make every inch count.

▼ An open shelf of plate racks and a spice rack that is mounted right above the stovetop keep often-used items readily at hand.

Rise Above

The kitchen is no place for wasting space. Every spare inch of vertical space—no matter how narrow—can be used to your advantage. An odd space that is just six to eight inches wide, for example, can hold serving trays or platters. You can also divide the area horizontally and use the narrow shelves for storing colorful towels and dishcloths, jars of spices or small serving pieces.

▲ Clever storage can create mini-stations in a kitchen. This serve-yourself area, located next to the coffeemaker, houses coffee, teas and other morning essentials.

▲ A single utensil drawer can become a storage powerhouse with the addition of double-tiered compartments on sliders.

▲ Spice drawer inserts with raised platforms keep spices from rolling around. They also make finding the jar you're looking for a snap.

▲ Storing items in baskets allows you to see when you need to replenish your stock of staples like onions and potatoes.

▶ Narrow vertical space is maximized here with a pull-out mini-pantry that can be accessed from two sides.

▲ Installing shallow, pull-out shelves in cabinets allows you to see contents easily and access only what you need.

▲ This handy unit—with pull-out shelves—may just inspire you to throw away your kitchen step stool!

▲ A built-in lazy Susan offers the convenience of easy access to frequently used items without wasting cabinet space.

▲ A full complement of knives and a pull-out cutting board beautifully blend the need for storage with a mini-prep center.

KITCHEN STYLES

Contemporary	Farmhouse
Cottage	French Country
Country	Modern
Craftsman	Old World
Eclectic	Rustic
Elegant	Traditional

finding your style

▲ An old-fashioned farmhouse-style sink with a gooseneck faucet that is mounted beneath granite countertops gives this kitchen an Old World style.

◀ Blending yesterday's charms with contemporary convenience, this new kitchen in a Martha's Vineyard home takes its cue from the island's century-old cottages by mixing old-fashioned style staples—open cabinetry, over-sized cupboards and a breakfast table with window bench—with modern amenities.

Style reflects your way of living. And these days one of the most lived-in rooms is the kitchen, where we gather and celebrate every day. So shouldn't it be the most beautifully designed room in the house?

Of course, this hardworking heart of the home needs to be efficient, but because it's where we spend so many of our waking hours, the kitchen should also be a place where our true personalities can shine. For some, this translates into a room imbued with an informal, country-like tone; others prefer a more contemporary atmosphere with sophisticated materials and appliances; and still others desire a one-of-a-kind setting that combines the best of several styles, achieved by mixing well-loved antiques with modern amenities.

Finding a style that evokes the mood you wish to create in your kitchen is a momentous decision. Choosing a style is the most exciting step in the kitchen process, setting the stage for everything that follows. Following your instincts when perusing kitchen styles allows your true preferences to emerge. Consistently responding to the warmth and intimacy of a cottage kitchen or gravitating to the sleek, cleaner design of a more modern space offers clues to what you ultimately want in a kitchen.

Considering how you use your kitchen also provides clues to styles that would best suit your needs. Some

▲ Style details like off-white speckled ceramic tile on the floors and backsplash and open white shelving filled with glassware and china add interest while softening the look of the stainless steel in this modern, commercial-style kitchen.

envision the perfect kitchen as the culinary command center for gourmet gatherings. Others picture a cozy, relaxed room for sharing intimate family meals. Imagining how you want your kitchen to perform can influence the way it should inevitably look. But determining your kitchen style isn't about absolutes. Many styles overlap and can easily be blended together to produce fantastic results. For instance, combining rustic elements in an elegant kitchen can add richness of detail; mix-

ing French country colors with a contemporary style can create a cheerful, functional space. Just as adding different ingredients to a favorite recipe makes it unique, the choices you make for your kitchen define the finished product, creating a look that truly reflects your own style. By visiting the gorgeous kitchens on the following pages—each packed with inspiration and examples of a variety of styles—you can define your preferences and explore exciting possibilities.

STYLE NOTES

Do Your Homework

To help define your style, fill a folder with images and notes culled from books, magazines and real homes. Keep a wish list of details and features for the kitchen of your dreams. Using your personal style to guide and inspire you will enable you to overcome any design challenge.

▶ A 1940s-era kitchen is brought up-to-date with stainless-steel work counters and restaurant appliances.

contemporary

▲ The arcing lines of twin islands provide plenty of prep space and add interest to the kitchen by playing curving lines against the angles of the sloping ceilings and linear cabinet doors.

Eschewing the formality of more traditional kitchens and the harder lines of modern design, contemporary style encourages flowing spaces and smart style that's both pretty and functional.

Contemporary kitchens can draw from a range of styles that evolved in the mid- to late-20th century. This style is known for softened or rounded lines and neutral elements teamed with accents of bold color.

Adopting a contemporary style in your own home can often mean creating separate but open activity zones or rethinking an out-of-date layout. For instance, many contemporary kitchens forgo a traditional dining room and

▶ In the breakfast nook, a wall of cabinets creates plenty of storage space for serving pieces and collectibles. It also features a desk area that any homeowner would covet.

▲ The kitchen's inner island houses the cooktop and provides seating for guests to join the cook during meal preparation.

▲ Frosted glass and pale maple cabinets give this kitchen an airy, contemporary feel.

instead employ a "great room" space that blends the kitchen, dining and family room spaces. The resulting open, airy design creates a style that looks spacious and up-to-date.

"Floating" island units also add a contemporary feel to an open-plan kitchen—and provide that extra bit of workspace that every chef dreams of.

▲ The outer island offers easy access to entertaining essentials, including a bar sink, a wine refrigerator and an ice maker.

▲ A breakfast bar makes quick work of kids' meals; stylish bar stools keep the look all grown-up.

◀ Diners enjoy an open view to the family room and its fireplace. The two spaces, which are separated by a bar with a sink, built-in ice maker and double-sided glass cabinets, allow for casual dining and post-meal conversation.

STYLE NOTES

Build Your Own

In lieu of a traditional dining set, many contemporary kitchens feature custom dining tables made from the same paneling and surfacing as cabinets and countertops. This approach gives the entire kitchen an in-sync, streamlined appearance that's both pleasing to the eye and practical. Duplicating countertop surfaces on a dining table often creates an additional durable work/prep space where guests can sit and help in meal preparation.

▲ Pale wood cabinets, creamy laminate countertops, warm-toned ceramic tile and stainless-steel appliances reflect light from the banks of windows that line this kitchen. A capacious center island, two sinks and an indoor grill are just the ticket for enjoying extended family gatherings.

▲ When space is limited and there's no room for a wall oven, opt for an above-range microwave with convection baking capability.

▲ Smart features in this kitchen include a flip-top bench by the side door, perfect for stowing boots under a cushioned top, and a planning desk in view of the dining area.

▲ A fully customized space, this contemporary kitchen is focused on utility and convenience. The well-lit island was built with varying counter heights to accommodate the reach of the two cooks in the house.

Light Effects

Contemporary kitchens are inherently bright and functional. Pendant lamps or recessed cans are often used to provide strong illumination for the island. Under-cabinet lighting shines on counter surfaces, and hidden up-lighting and perimeter spotlights highlight decorative items while banishing dark corners.

▶ Cabinets in a pickled maple finish, cream-colored walls and planks of solid ash flooring stained in a golden hue create a soothing neutral background.

▲ Stylish storage abounds in this well-designed kitchen. Mini alcoves on either side of the range put spices, sauces and condiments in easy reach. The island includes attractive wine storage for 26 bottles and a corner cabinet to hold favorite cooking tomes.

▲ Clean lines are achieved in this kitchen with built-in appliances and cabinets dedicated to housing small appliances. A heavy-duty mixer and food processor mounted on spring-loaded shelves swing out and lock at counter height for easy use.

▲ Dazzling details make all the difference. The massive stone arch surround for the recessed range is actually made from cultured stone that measures just two inches thick. Textured metallic tiles create a reflective surface that gives the kitchen a warm glow.

cottage

◀ Blending familiar items in unexpected ways, such as using a ladder as a decorative element, is a signature of cottage style.

Whimsical, unpretentious and utterly charming, cottage style has become an increasingly popular choice for the kitchen.

Life in a cottage embodies the appeal of a snug, simple life in surroundings that are cozy and intimate—the antithesis of bigger spaces that can often feel empty. Reminiscent of summers at the beach or the lake, the cot-

tage style is usually exemplified by furnishings and decor that are cheerful, artistic and comfortably familiar.

Staples of cottage interiors include weathered finishes, simple whites and beadboard on the walls and cabinets juxtaposed with fresh colors inspired by rambling wildflower gardens.

This style can create a mood that's romantic, funky or quaint—it all

depends on how you interpret the style. The cottage look is especially effective for cooks who want to create a kitchen that doesn't take itself too seriously, but want guests to feel as if they've stumbled onto something both special and welcoming.

This fun and light style encourages "accidental decorating," such as a mix-and-match collection of antiques, flea market finds, artworks and handi-crafts. The end result is a carefree mood and a look that reflects the essence of nature and simplicity.

▼ Tucked away under a handsome hood, a cheerful blue Viking range is a perfect match for the sun and moon tile backsplash. Humble gingham curtains reinforce the cottage look, and an antique sailing ornament made into a hanging light plays up this home's waterfront location.

▶ With hefty drawers for stashing spices and utensils, this furniture-like island mimics the look of an antique table while serving as the room's functional centerpiece.

Create Cottage Appeal

CREATE A SHOWCASE. Let neutral cabinetry show off colorful accessories, like glazed pottery, antique dishcloths or a tin vase filled with a wildflower bouquet. Rotate items from other rooms to prevent the display from becoming stale.

LAYER COLOR. Echo the hues of the kitchen's color scheme with artwork, fresh flowers, candles, countertop surfaces and other bright accents.

CREATE COTTAGE CHIC. Bring a window-box garden of herbs indoors. Choose wicker or mix-and-match chairs rather than a traditional kitchen set, and don't be afraid to add the unexpected—like a rocking chair. Whitewashed walls, gingham cafe curtains and an open pantry or glass-front cabinets are just some ways to make a cottage kitchen lively.

▶ A large cabinet designed to resemble a free-standing armoire shows off a collection of favorite antique china that echoes the room's color scheme.

▲ Small on space but big on personality, a San Francisco cottage kitchen gets character from an artful rainbow of colorful dishware and accessories. In the tradition of Warhol, a simple row of canned stewed tomatoes makes a strong style statement.

◀ A well-loved butcher-block table is worked into this kitchen design as an airy replacement for a traditional island.

▶ Custom-designed windows and light finishes create a sun-drenched workspace.

country

▲ Today's relaxed country kitchen exemplifies an "unfitted" look. Some cabinets are constructed with dark-stained cherry wood while others are painted maple. Both have been carefully distressed and glazed to create a warm, welcoming atmosphere.

Country kitchens have always been popular for their inviting nature and conduciveness to cheerful, close-knit family gatherings. Though they are most often characterized by simple furniture, muted colors, milk-paint finishes and homespun or classic fabrics, today's country-style kitchens are open to even broader interpretation. The country style continues to evolve with updated looks that evoke a mood that's both homey and casual, yet stresses clean lines.

Soft tones, painted cabinets and warm tile accents account for much of country style's continuing charm. Also in sync with the essence of this style is the popular trend of mixing like-styled cabinetry in different finishes, as well as incorporating a variety of materials that encourage visitors to kick back and enjoy the surroundings.

More than just a pretty picture, a country kitchen can also be high on function. Although historic in appearance, new cabinets and kitchen "furni-

▶ An eye-catching ceramic platter is mortared into the tiled wall, creating a one-of-a-kind, three-dimensional effect.

ture" in the country style are designed to look old-fashioned while offering plenty of storage and convenience options. The addition of glass-front cabinetry and open shelving, a hallmark of the style, is perfect for showcasing mixing bowls, teapots and other country staples. An open design akin to a country great room allows for family and guests to interact with the cook. Potted plants, country-style wooden chairs with comfortable cushions and a large table for hearty meals reinforce the style's practical sensibilities.

▼ In the country tradition, food preparation is a family affair. The design here includes two separate sinks, allowing two sets of hands to wash dishes and prep vegetables simultaneously.

▶ A handsome apron-style sink with a decorative facade and a deep, functional basin echoes this kitchen's sophisticated country theme.

▲ Details add a lot to this kitchen, like this deep, square, artistic prep sink. It coordinates with the decorative plate above the cooktop, creating an overall look of country chic. Note the sink's vintage-style, one-handle fixture.

Country Accents

INJECT PERSONALITY. Put your own personal stamp on the wallspace between the cooktop and the hood. Display something unique to infuse your kitchen with character, such as mosaic tiles, a colorful trompe l'oeil bowl of fruit or a tiny window.

MAKE IT LIGHT. Country kitchens are cheery and bright. Lighting doesn't need to match, but it should suit the room. For example, you can pair a rusted-finish, utilitarian light over the work island with a graceful chandelier or pendant lamp in the dining area.

GIVE PATTERNS A FRESH LOOK. Bring a more updated country feel to windows by pairing a botanical print with a solid-color fabric and raise the level of the tiebacks, as shown here.

SHOWCASE KITCHEN STAPLES. Shiny copper pots hung by their handles on a wall or an interesting collection of wooden utensils in a milk-glass vase are just two ways you can keep these kitchen staples handy, while creating minute works of art that complement your country style.

▶ There's no need to camouflage structural elements like the beams in this kitchen. They add dramatic impact while playing up the country style. Split islands that invite movement are divided by a practical tile aisle, which picks up the colors of the tactile volcanic-ash countertops.

Tweaking Tradition

FIND YOUR FAVORITE. Calico fabrics with patterns in delicate florals, gingham checks or clean and simple stripes enliven an understated country style.

GIVE COUNTRY A KICK. Muted, time-worn hues are typical of traditional country, but infusing small accents of red, black or bright white can give country a more contemporary feel.

ADD HANDMADE APPEAL. Accents and accessories that look like they've been handcrafted reinforce the country style. Wicker or woven baskets, wooden bowls, crockery and pewter or copper pieces also complement the style.

◀ Exposed beams, hanging pots and warm wood floors play off the clean lines of a stainless-steel refrigerator, showing how a country design can be injected with modern conveniences without losing its appeal.

▼ A quaint breakfast table by a window with a wooded view captures the mood of a weekend in the country. It also provides an intimate space for eating and relaxing.

craftsman

▲ Sunlight and open spaces play a major role in this kitchen. The large soapstone-topped island and gleaming stainless-steel appliances balance the natural tones found elsewhere in the room.

Craftsman style, which is also known as Arts and Crafts or Mission, became popular in the early 1900s, when Americans grew tired of the decorative excesses of the Victorian era. Craftsman emerged as a more informal approach to decorating with practical built-ins, open living spaces warmed by a central fireplace and a deliberate lack of ornamentation.

Glorifying craftsmanship in its simple shapes with exposed joinery, spare ornamentation and strong lines,

Craftsman also became known for its heavy emphasis on natural materials. Architectural details that make the Craftsman style so appealing include exposed beams, built-in furniture and an emphasis on stone, cedar and metal.

With interior wood surfaces that are stained rather than painted to emphasize the beautiful wood grain, Craftsman conveys warmth, workmanship and an unmistakable sense of home and hearth—qualities that translate perfectly into kitchen style.

STYLE NOTES

Get Crafty

Elements such as simple plate racks, hand-forged hardware and solid hardwood furniture that has straight lines and is free of fancy veneers are at home in a Craftsman kitchen. Examples of this style can be found among antique or reproduction pieces inspired by Gustav Stickley, an original manufacturer of furniture in the Craftsman style.

▲ Custom cherry cabinets with lots of wood grain detail, clear fir trim and silky soapstone countertops create an organic look and tactile appeal in this gourmet haven.

▲ A simple breakfast nook built into a windowed corner gives this kitchen an intimate, hand-hewn quality. Attention to detail, such as the carvings on the table support and the warmth of the surrounding woodwork, create a distinct Craftsman look.

▲ The formal dining area opens onto the kitchen. Fir trim around the windows and custom-made furniture reinforce the Craftsman styling of the house.

eclectic

▲ A once-dark kitchen is enlivened by blending elements of Tuscan, retro and rustic styles. An updated antique library-style cabinet creates the room's one-of-a-kind work island.

At its most effective, eclectic design is the conscious combination of various materials, elements and themes that blend beautifully to create one-of-a-kind style.

If you love the results you get from breaking the rules, drawing from different periods or mixing elements of one style with another, eclectic design can be very rewarding.

Things that might clash in other surroundings blend beautifully in eclectic style, which brings together colors, shapes, textures and finishes in unexpected ways. Just follow your instincts: Juxtaposing an unusual combination of finishes and blending treasures, heirlooms and other collectibles with more modern trappings can set an eclectic kitchen apart from the rest.

▶ Create "instant architecture" by adding surprise elements, like these ornamental wrought-iron brackets and old wood beams that frame the modern stainless-steel range and hood.

▲ A fresh palette of appealing, muted earth tones threads together a bounty of complex materials. Architect-designed cabinetry with antique wire-mesh door inserts and a small soapstone counter make this area unique.

◀ A second sink, this time made of beefy soapstone and surrounded by a hefty concrete counter, offers a serious work/prep space while reinforcing the kitchen's mixed-material aesthetic.

▶ Dual skylights and a dramatic, arched, triple-casement window bring natural light into this kitchen, adding a bright glow to the muted color scheme and softening the hard lines of the ceiling.

More so than with any other design style, choosing eclectic style is a labor of love, because it is so personal. Eclectic style encourages collectors to showcase items like salvaged architectural pieces and antique tiles, interesting craftsmanship and, of course, their own creativity.

In an eclectic kitchen, it's easy to find a home for a favorite antique or vintage piece, or to allow a piece of furniture, fabric or artwork to become the inspiration for an entire room. The best way to make an eclectic kitchen sing is to include a few or more of your favorite things.

▼ Bold pieces, like an 1800s marble fireplace surround, a blue Deco mirror and an array of colorful art glass, define the style of this eclectic kitchen. The island's furniture-like details and the handsome millwork throughout pay tribute to craftsmanship.

▶ Fanciful hanging lamps procured from an old ice cream parlor draw the eye up to the room's high ceilings and arched French doors while setting off the surface of the island's salvaged blue Bahia marble.

▶ A cooking area gets attitude from out-of-the-ordinary antique tiles, including Minton peacocks dating back to the 1800s and well-dressed ladies circa 1950. Another novelty is the use of vintage glass hardware on cabinets, which complements the lightness of the white marble countertops and appliances.

elegant

▲ A tumbled marble backsplash and granite countertops bring a regal feeling to this kitchen. Intricate moldings and display shelves were all custom-made to add a touch of classic elegance.

Replete in augmentation and embellishments, elegant kitchens create a feast for the eyes. Every little detail—from ornate cabinetry features to handsome hardware—combines to create a setting that's graceful, well designed and pleasing to the eye.

Elaborate window treatments, wallpaper, handmade rugs, candelabras or a silver tea service are some of the elements that can turn any kitchen into an elegant space. In some elegant kitchens, the dining area and surrounding space serves the function of a second dining room, formal enough to be the focus of entertaining.

But whether a kitchen is imbued with casual elegance or more formal in nature, it doesn't have to sacrifice functionality. Striking appliances and the latest conveniences are at home in an elegant kitchen. In most cases they are camouflaged by custom cabinetry and built-in looks, and paired with rich textures of stone, granite and marble to create a look that blends in seamlessly.

STYLE NOTES

Accessorize

Elegant kitchens can feature accessories such as classic still-life oils of fruit, antique sconces or chandeliers. Oriental throw rugs and/or window treatments with a tailored look also add appeal.

Richness in Details

PAINT WITH COLOR. White rooms tend to look stark and modern. To make your room look elegant, opt instead for rich hues.

BUILD UP ARCHITECTURE. Installing moldings to ceilings and around doors and windows adds visual interest and character. Using columns to frame a breakfast area or arches over a sink or range creates a classic, timeless effect.

▲ In addition to granite countertops, the butcher block atop the island provides a second work surface that's a perfect place for rolling dough. An arched shelf for cookbooks and latticework wine storage play off the room's elaborate moldings, including fluting, roping and corbels.

▲ Dangling crystals on a wrought-iron candle chandelier add to this kitchen's dramatic appeal.

▲ Red wallpaper and tailored window treatments with tassel pulls are juxtaposed with simple, fine furniture to create a breakfast area that's elegant, but not stuffy.

◀ Practical features to suit a gourmet chef—such as an oversized work island and the 42-inch professional-style range with two ovens—merge seamlessly with the fleur-de-lis tile backsplash and a finely crafted mantelpiece above the range, which conceals a high-powered ventilation hood.

Gracious Additions

Adding built-ins such as cushioned window benches and bookcases brings a touch of Old World elegance to any kitchen. A butler's pantry is also a useful and attractive addition. Typically located between the kitchen and the dining room, this area is perfect for last-minute prepping of food platters and for storing extra service pieces within easy reach.

▼ Arched glass-paned doors adorn the front of the built-in hutch, which mimics the look of an heirloom china cabinet. It features an ornate European ogee edge that is repeated on the granite countertops.

▲ Materials with an aged appearance and classically styled cabinets with pewter knobs and drawer pulls create this elegant enclave. Cabinet doors with an aged white finish, raised panels, and exposed hinges mimic the style of antique furniture.

▲ Custom cabinetry with elegant details and moldings provides plenty of specialized storage—such as the wine rack and appliance garage—while camouflaging essentials like the exhaust hood above the cooktop.

▲ Everything from the richly coffered ceiling to the delicately scrolled brackets that support the top of the rounded island exudes casual elegance in this kitchen.

farmhouse

To maintain a view of the kitchen's focal point—an original exposed stone wall—the island cooktop was created with a built-in downdraft ventilation unit instead of an overhead hood.

Traditional country that embraces modern elements creates the look of today's farmhouse style. Inspired by the clean lines of farmhouse architecture, this style features open spaces and classic charm blended with modern professional materials and up-to-the-minute amenities.

Farmhouse style lends itself to furniture that appears handcrafted. Hefty wooden farmhouse tables that can seat large groups comfortably are at home in this style, which conjures up images of freshly collected eggs and sitting down to a hearty country breakfast—even if the kitchen is located in the confines of the city. By engaging in a deft mix of old and new, this fresh country approach creates an effect of timeless, comforting style.

▶ Specialized storage like this wine rack helps keep order in the kitchen.

▲ The kitchen takes its inspiration from the formal dining room of this 18th-century farmhouse, complete with an enormous stone fireplace.

▲ Decorative details and accent pieces add dimension to create a pulled-together look.

▲ This kitchen features a variety of finishes used to brilliant effect. Painted cabinets in a deep blue-green hue stand out against the natural wood flooring, island and antique cabinet. White solid surfacing brightens the room, as does the kitchen's ceiling. This was achieved by painting the exposed beams white without losing their architectural appeal.

▲ Roughly hewn beams frame the workspace of this farmhouse kitchen and separate it from the dining area. An Italian crackled tile backsplash complements the limed oak cabinets and contrasts beautifully with the Dakota mahogany granite surface. Stainless-steel appliances give the room an updated, modern edge.

Create Farmhouse Chic

Go beyond traditional storage options and look for farm-friendly alternatives. Add rectangular wicker bins or wire baskets for smart storage; display mason jars, copper molds and cast-iron cookware; and consider glass or wire-mesh fronts for cabinet doors.

▶ French doors just beyond the breakfast nook offer great views as well as easy access to a patio for added entertaining space.

Light and Welcoming

ENHANCE YOUR VIEWS. Country kitchens should provide a window to nature. Replace or reposition windows that are unsightly or not in keeping with the kitchen style.

ACHIEVE A BRIGHT OUTLOOK. A room that lacks natural sunlight can be brightened by the sparkle of reflective stainless-steel appliances, simple white walls and white solid surfacing on counters.

MIX AND MATCH. Prevent kitchens from looking too stark by augmenting white with a variety of finishes. Mixing woods in a country style—either by using two different finishes on cabinets or adding a hutch or farmhouse table in wood alongside painted cabinets—gives the room a historical feel.

▲ Open cabinet shelves and glass doors suit the architecture of this airy, one-story home. This dishwasher is one of two in the kitchen, speeding cleanup after parties.

▲ Comfort and simplicity rule in this kitchen, where seating at the bar affords guests a beautiful view of the farm outside the kitchen windows.

french country

▲ Open cabinetry, glass-paneled doors and the European flavor of blue-and-white tiles bring a light touch to this kitchen.

French country style, characterized by practicality and simple elegance, takes its roots from Provence. While known for pieces that have the humble appeal of handcrafted peasant furniture or natural woodwork, the French country color scheme is the style's best-known characteristic. Intense, bold hues like sea blue, sunny yellow, leaf green and crisp, clean whites figure prominently in this style, as do materials like stone, terra-cotta, copper and wrought iron.

Although it sounds very specific, French country style can have many interpretations. Radiating warmth and rural grace, French country kitchens can include rustic architectural features, such as exposed ceiling beams, rough stone floors or rough plaster walls. Grapes, roosters, vines and sunflowers also figure prominently in this decor. Other motifs depicted in French country accessories are farmyards, countryside scenes or pastoral landscapes, as well as toile patterns, checks

▲ Authentic features like an imported copper sink with graceful gooseneck faucet and dainty porcelain handles lend this kitchen loads of charm.

▲ Bathed in eternal sunshine—courtesy of color-washed walls that create a warm glow—and utilizing materials and antiques indicative of Provence, this kitchen easily replicates the feeling of a farmhouse kitchen in the South of France.

▲ A built-in island separates the kitchen from the breakfast table, encouraging convivial gatherings. The stunning effect on the walls was created with layers of paint and glaze applied with gauze.

and stripes. The crowning touch to a classic French country kitchen is the addition of a cozy stone hearth, complete with iron tools, copper pots, hanging dried herbs and the comfort of a roaring fire.

Sophisticated and endearing, French country can mimic the look of elegant estates in the French countryside or charming cottages in the Provençal tradition. A kitchen decorated in this style can easily be updated by simply choosing different accent colors, motifs or accessories to create an inviting, interesting appearance. Timeless and well-established, a French country kitchen can weather the years and the changing tides of taste.

▲ Glass-fronted cabinetry and a color palette inspired by the hues of sea and sand keep this kitchen looking bright and open.

▼ With its cheerful and bright appearance, this charming kitchen beautifully evokes the sentiment of French country style. It features hallmarks such as terra-cotta tile and an iron pot rack modeled after one seen by the owners while vacationing in Provence.

To create a French country look, breakfast-table chairs were treated to a fresh coat of paint and a distressed finish, while existing cabinetry was updated with a glaze to create a well-loved appearance.

▲ The cabinets were given an opaque stain that resembles a painted finish and a recessed inset door that allows for architectural details like molding and beadboard paneling. Dishes in the open shelves add a French accent.

▶ A country-style hutch with antique dishes, along with painted dining room chairs, echoes the blue-and-white color scheme of the kitchen.

▲ Charming and flooded with light—thanks to an oversized arched window and reflective white cabinets—this kitchen exemplifies the simple appeal of French country.

▲ A pleasing palette of crisp white and bright yellow brings warmth to the L-shaped workspace. Simple, unadorned accessories complete the modern picture.

Simple, streamlined, more functional than fussy. These are the characteristics of successfully executed modern style. Crisp and organized—with an appreciation of geometry and asymmetry—modern style is especially exciting in a kitchen, where it offers a look that's both fresh and familiar.

Elements of modern style include gleaming metal, sleek cabinetry and smooth surfaces. Concrete, granite and linoleum are popular flooring choices. Chrome and stainless-steel pro-style appliances that pair high performance with attractive design are also in sync with modern sensibilities.

▶ An unobtrusive sideboard-style cabinet in the dining area offers ample, concealed storage. The airy, open feeling and extra light from windows and doors free of treatments is in keeping with the modern look.

The clean lines of the large island provide an oasis of calm, an uncluttered space to sit and visit during meal preparation.

For many, the appeal of modern style is the chance to incorporate the latest in high-tech gadgets and conveniences that can bring a room up to speed, improve functionality and allow for multitasking. The addition of extra sinks, laptop computers, drop-down flat-screen TVs and other bells and whistles can make a modern style kitchen that much more enjoyable.

Whether a home is 70 years old or seven, a modern kitchen can easily blend in to the space, complementing the rooms that surround it. Since the advent of appliances, the kitchen has easily been the most modern room in a home. In fact, it's not unusual at all for the style of a kitchen to be cutting edge and years ahead of the other rooms in the house.

▶ The spare, neat nature of modern styling often produces a look of simple elegance. Mixing woods creates an edgy, modern ambiance with natural-colored maple cabinets complemented by the cherry stools. An adjacent dining space does double duty with the addition of a built-in entertainment center and well-organized work desk.

▼ Modern conveniences include no-nonsense, industrial-style stainless-steel appliances (including an extra wall oven for baking) and a marble-topped prep island with two sinks. Ribbed glass cabinet fronts enhance the room's neat, streamlined appearance.

◄ A powerful hose spray for washing produce or blasting dirty dishes is an enticing extra.

Modern Advantages

If you have the space, consider features that will add convenience and luxury to your kitchen. For example, a temperature-controlled wine refrigerator is about the size of a dishwasher; the best models feature tinted glass doors to filter out harmful rays while still permitting viewing. If wine storage is not essential, adding a second, smaller refrigerator away from the work triangle lets guests help themselves to beverages.

▼ A modern stainless-steel cook's kitchen makes the most of limited space by incorporating a work island that doubles as a dining table. Even with its shiny steel and high-tech efficiency, the space generates a warm, friendly vibe with open shelves showcasing a neat collection of colorful dishes and glassware.

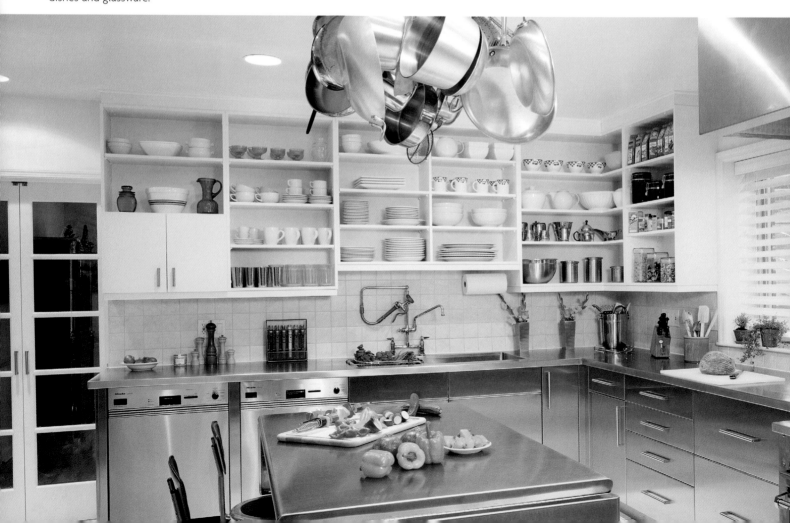

▲ Natural materials, intersecting angles and broad curves direct the eye around the workspace of this modern yet warm kitchen. A bold, gleaming stainless-steel range hood was designed to be the focal point of the room.

▲ Full-slide drawers pull all the way out, allowing the cook to view the complete contents of each drawer from front to back without crouching on the floor.

▲ Creating a kitchen-as-command-center feeling, the galley-shaped workspace, with its open layout, is designed to appear larger than it is.

old world

▲ Moss-colored solid surfacing on counters is broken up with a vintage apron-style porcelain sink.

◀ Open shelves filled with collectibles conjure up images of Grandma's old-fashioned kitchen. A modern stainless-steel fridge beside the shelves looks classic in this setting.

A kitchen that embraces the Old World style is unmistakable. In its fine points and design, it honors historic heritage and brings back classic elements from the past that aren't necessarily commonplace. Whether it's filled with architectural details, vintage-look appliances and furniture-quality cabinetry (or actual antiques and salvaged treasures), entering an Old World kitchen creates a feeling of history, a look that manages to appear timeless, yet timely.

Old World kitchens call to mind a special ambiance, a look that is anything but mass-produced. Cabinetry possesses a one-of-a-kind quality, fine craftsmanship and a gracious nod to times of simple elegance. Architectural features, some old, some designed to look that way, reinforce Old World sensibility and embrace old-fashioned charm and character. Plastered walls, carved woodwork and cabinetry with an artisan's attention to detail are celebrated. The use of original, salvaged

▶ Cabinets with open toekicks look freestanding, a detail not found in contemporary cabinetry styles. Glass-front cabinets and decorative metal drawer pulls have a decidedly retro feel, as does the range.

pieces in a kitchen sets the room apart, lending special credibility to Old World style. Yet even with a centuries-old look, modern 21st-century conveniences can still be easily adapted to fit today's Old World style.

Stay True to History

When replacing worn-out elements in your kitchen, select pieces that complement your home's original architecture. Pay attention to period hardware on doors and use that to guide kitchen hardware choices.

▶ Timeless design elements, such as the custom-made range hood (bronze treated to create instant patina), the limestone counters and floors, and the crown molding that runs from the kitchen into the formal dining room, create the illusion of a kitchen that has been here for 100 years.

▼ Showcasing old-fashioned charm and detailing on a grand scale, the frame-style cabinetry with inset doors and drawers painted in gleaming white lacquer has an Old World appearance. There's not a single exposed hinge to mar its surface.

Old World Aesthetic

FIND YOUR FOCAL POINT. Start with an antique or salvaged piece and then work around it. It's almost impossible to find a treasure and then try to introduce it into an existing design. The scale and proportion will invariably look "off," taking impact away from the piece you wanted to showcase.

THINK NATURAL. Surfaces can be either smooth or distressed for a time-worn look, but above all they should be natural. Solid surfacing or laminate has no place in an Old World kitchen. Tumbled marble and granite are perfect choices.

USE PERIOD LIGHTING. Sconces and chandeliers with metal finishes are more appropriate than recessed cans.

SHOW YOUR CURVES. Standout features in an Old World-styled home include arched doorways and windows, as well as curved or rippled pillars.

CHOOSE A SUBTLE PALETTE. Muted colors and textured walls that look time aged or are faux finished for an antique look suit this style best.

◀ Designed around a salvaged Victorian hutch that inspired the room's cabinetry, this new kitchen looks anything but modern. To fit the room, the hutch was split in two and installed on either side of the breakfast nook. The English balance light (so-called because it can be raised or lowered using a weighted balance system) over the breakfast table is an authentic original.

▲ Affecting a step-back-in-time appearance required an eye for detail. Older elements of the design inspire some brand-new features. The light fixture over the island, for example, is a new reproduction of an older piece; only its shades are antique.

▲ Wide-plank wood floors, painted wood cabinets, beautifully detailed glass doors and period light fixtures fool the eye into thinking this kitchen was crafted in the mid-1800s. A capacious island with farmhouse sink and gooseneck faucet offers plenty of surface area for food prep and buffet-style entertaining.

▲ Bare windows pay homage both to spectacular views outside and to the beauty of the woodwork indoors. Two dishwashers, on either side of the double sink, ensure easy cleanup when entertaining.

Warm, woodsy and always inviting, the rustic style takes its cue from nature and evokes the mood of rural retreats, such as ski cabins, Western ranches and rough-and-tumble Adirondack lodges. The beauty of nature comes alive in kitchens imbued with rustic style, defined by natural materials and a color palette that leans heavily on earthy hues.

Stone, rough-hewn wood beams and the bold use of aged metals distinguish rustic from other styles. Rather than opting for modern conveniences and high-tech accoutrements, the rustic kitchen places an emphasis on simplicity of design and efficient use of space to achieve maximum functionality.

Rustic kitchens can range from spare to casual to all-out elegant, but the prevailing mood the style creates is one of an escape to something more peaceful, primitive and organic. But don't let all the natural beauty fool you—a rustic kitchen is sturdy enough to endure the test of time.

▶ Exposed Douglas fir ceiling beams, a 125-year-old terra-cotta floor and the deeply burnished patina on a custom-built copper and iron ventilation hood all conjure images of the American West. The center of the kitchen, a work island crafted from knotty wood, has a built-in refrigerator, affording guests the freedom to help themselves.

▲ A sturdy wood table with a whimsical antique wooden bench situated by the warmth of the stone fireplace provides a cozy spot for breaking bread.

▶ Although more formal in nature, this kitchen, located in a mountain retreat, draws elements directly from nature. Rustic finishes include a tumbled marble backsplash highlighted by stone, a patchwork floor of slate in earthy hues, a verdant green granite countertop and a wrought-iron wall sculpture.

◀ Attention to detail, like the roughly hewn appeal of this hammered copper sink basin, adds richness to the room's rustic style.

Exposed Elements

ROUGH IT UP. The texture of rough plaster and the impact of exposed brick, rock or stone walls and wooden beams are all elements that can contribute to the rustic style.

OPEN IT UP. Opt for vaulted high ceilings to bring the airy feeling of outdoors inside. Bare windows or the simplest of window treatments suit the rustic style, encouraging open views and unfiltered natural light.

MIX IN METALS. Wrought-iron accents and accessories like candles, lantern-like sconces and stools or chairs with sturdy metal legs reinforce the rustic theme. A showcase of utilitarian metal objects, such as colanders or copper pots, makes a decorative statement.

KEEP IT NATURAL. Bent willow, reed or hickory furniture complements a rustic kitchen, as do accessories that feature worn leather, distressed wood and twig or log accents.

▶ A built-in hutch to the left of the range stores earthenware and other collectibles within view. Panels in the drawers showcase a harvest rainbow of beans and pasta.

▼ Besides adding unique architecture, a stone wall showcases both a fireplace and raised television that can be seen and enjoyed in the kitchen and the adjacent family room.

▲ Mellow maple wood cabinets with fine detailing and a soaring vaulted ceiling link this updated kitchen to a sunny dining room addition.

Traditional kitchens evoke feelings of the familiar by adroitly drawing on elements from the past. Although clearly modernized in appearance, these kitchens create a mood that recalls a traditional sense of time and space.

Mixing classic and contemporary elements, traditional kitchens can be imbued with modern sophistication and sensibilities, yet still appeal to more conservative tastes. Creating an atmosphere that is functional and high performance without appearing so, traditional kitchens take on more of a look that's furnished and finely crafted.

Sleek surfaces are balanced with warm woodwork and soft lines, non-

▶ As seen from the dining area, prints and tapestries decorating the kitchen and adjoining den are in sync with the room's traditional good looks.

Lit by Tiffany-style pendant lamps, the granite-topped work island, which doubles as a snack bar, features traditional carved open woodwork above a niche for shelving. A simple slate backsplash in a diamond pattern complements the detailed woodwork without competing.

essentials are stowed away discretely rather than displayed and beautiful details abound without overpowering. Other elements in a traditional kitchen can include classic dining tables with traditional seating, windows covered with curtains or valances and rich wood cabinetry.

▶ Classic touches, like the Palladian window over the sink, echo the arches of the glass-fronted cabinets on either side of it. A lovely beveled edge on the granite countertops recalls furniture details of a bygone era.

▼ Details delight in this traditional kitchen with a twist. Finely detailed, furniture-style cabinetry jazzed up with a striking washed blue finish makes the biggest statement of all. Matching cabinet panels on the appliances shroud these kitchen workhorses in a sophisticated guise.

▲ A built-in hutch comprised of cabinetry across from the dining area mimics the look of freestanding furniture. An informal dining area is perfect for breakfast and other casual meals.

▲ Warm hues and diverse materials, such as an eye-catching strip of terra-cotta tiles lining the oven hood, add richness and texture to this kitchen.

▲ A richly hued runner complements the blue cabinets in this kitchen and provides warmth underfoot. Polished oak floors to match the rest of the home lend a traditional look. To create an open floor plan while maintaining a more traditional, formal look, a work island, part of the original kitchen design, was eliminated.

▲ A marriage of modern and traditional elements, this kitchen blends traditional details like crown moldings with the "wow" factor of a ceramic tile backsplash with a metallic finish. Guests can pull up a bar stool and chat with the cook at a 42-inch-high island—designed to hide messy dishes, pots and pans on the opposite side.

◀ Under-cabinet lights ease tasks and highlight surfaces. At night the black granite displays green and gold flecks, and the accent strip's pressed metal tile forms a beautiful basket-weave effect.

Frosted glass inserts add visual interest to the warm maple cabinets. A checkerboard tile floor is updated with glass mosaic copper-finished inserts. The timeless look of stainless steel on the built-in refrigerator and double oven contributes to the kitchen's overall inviting appearance.

▲ Facilitating the kitchen's tidy appearance is a built-in desk flanked by two roomy, pantry-like closets equipped with roll-out shelves and bins.

▲ Flowing naturally off the kitchen, a sunny breakfast room sports the same palette of soothing colors, including decoratively painted and textured walls. Convenient open shelves, stationed here and there, provide easy access to favorite ceramics, family pictures and books.

DETAILS, DETAILS, DETAILS

◀ Smart stainless-steel handles link this kitchen's cabinetry with its appliances and light fixtures.

cabinet smarts

▲ A sparkling white finish on cabinetry lends a cheerful note to this kitchen's darker-hued walls and floors.

Although utilitarian in nature, cabinetry is one of the key decorative elements of any kitchen. Besides gracefully storing all of your essentials, cabinetry defines a kitchen's overall look, setting the tone and the mood for everything that follows. Outfitting a kitchen with rich, cherry, Arts and Crafts-inspired cabinetry creates a warm enclave, while a kitchen featuring painted-white cabinetry evokes crisp, country appeal.

The design impact of cabinetry has resulted in more available options, including elaborate moldings, hand-carved details, distressed looks or a spare, slick, modern finish. In addition to wood, other cabinet materials used to great effect include aluminum, stainless steel and laminates. You can even combine two or more cabinetry finishes to create an eclectic look. No matter which style you choose, cabinetry will commandeer most of the wall space in a kitchen and take the biggest chunk out of your budget, so it's important to choose wisely.

There are many things to consider before you make any decisions. Visiting home design retailers and taking notes on what you like and dislike is a great first step. Identifying details of cabinet styles you admire can help narrow your search immediately. Once you have an idea of what you like, it's easier to zero in on specifics.

buying basics

Before you allow yourself to become swept away by the beautiful cabinet choices that are currently available, do some homework.

Prioritize your needs. Do you want to maximize storage space or are you just ready for a new look? For inspiration, look through magazines, visit manufacturers' web sites and request product brochures. Cabinet stores, home centers and showrooms will have displays that feature various materials, finishes and detailing. There's no substitute for seeing the product in person.

Know your materials. Cabinets can be built from solid woods such as oak, cherry, pine, walnut or maple. These cabinets are durable, but can be expensive. They are mostly used in custom construction. Most cabinets are made from wood composites and faced with wood veneer, laminate or metal. These give the same effect as solid wood, but at a much lower cost. You can also opt for solid wood doors on cabinet boxes made from composites or plywood.

Be savvy about "custom." Custom cabinets are built to fit exact specifications, including style, size and storage requirements. As with custom-made products, you can have exactly what you want made to your order by a cabinetmaker or in a woodworking shop. But the cost will be higher than for stock cabinets. With semi-custom, you can have cabinetry made to your order in a factory. Choosing from the manufacturer's selection of materials, sizes, finishes and styles can save you money.

Consider "stock" options. Stock cabinets are ready-to-ship styles that allow designers to combine a variety of preconstructed units to fit just about any space. These work best for budget-conscious renovators. Many designers can achieve a customized look with stock cabinetry simply by the way they arrange them. Other "customizing" techniques used with stock cabinets include painting, adding moldings or upgrading the hardware.

▼ Elegant, cream-colored cabinetry is the star of this kitchen. The glass doors, which showcase china, and a furniture-quality island serve as two stunning focal points.

▲ Two cabinet finishes blend together to create a distinctive look in this modern kitchen. Pairing light and dark together makes for a striking combination.

▲ A painted, aged finish is the perfect fit for a kitchen with Old World appeal.

▲ To add texture and design interest to the streamlined wall cabinets, the doors were fitted with glass overlaid in perforated metal. Another surprising element is the use of stainless-steel top drawers in the base cabinets instead of wood.

▲ Pay attention to storage extras, such as plate racks, trays, lazy Susan shelves and drawer dividers. Consider these extras within the context of the items you need to store. Items like cutlery trays, spice racks and storage bins are easier to work into your kitchen design at the inception.

F ine points matter when it comes to cabinetry. The little details will add to both function and style.

For example, cabinets can be framed or frameless. Face-framed cabinets, a more traditional look, have a support around the front of the cabinet, creating the appearance of a frame around the door. Frameless models feature a doweled construction. This allows the doors to fit flush with the cabinet box and creates a more contemporary, European look.

Cabinet doors are also available in a spectrum of styles, from traditional to country to contemporary. And your options don't end there. You can choose from a multitude of construction options, including raised-panel squares, raised-panel Roman arches, raised-panel classic arches, recessed panels, Shaker style and much more.

Once you've chosen a door style, natural choices in terms of finish and decorative hardware become evident. Choose a finish that complements the construction material you've chosen. For instance, a finish that appears distressed or softly color washed works well with farmhouse-style cabinetry. To further augment doors, there are endless possibilities from panels and moldings to the addition of other materials, such as glass doors or metallic inserts.

No matter how it looks, cabinetry is more than just a pretty face. Behind those stylish drawers and doors are the actual storage areas—called boxes— with shelves behind the doors and

◀ A popular cabinet detail is a look that mimics fine furniture with decorative moldings and carved feet or legs at the base. Furniture styling allows you to complement your existing decor and give your space a more personal flair.

◀ Display spaces like these storage cubbies offer a handy spot for frequently used items. Installing shelves to showcase favorite dishware and collectibles has the added benefit of keeping them accessible.

STYLE NOTES

Mix & Match

Creating an "unfitted" kitchen is a popular alternative to the streamlined look of built-in cabinets. An unfitted style, achieved by using freestanding cabinets and cupboards or built-in cabinetry at varied cabinet heights and placements, has an old-fashioned appeal. Many custom and semi-custom collections include unfitted pieces, such as food-preparation islands made in woods and finishes to match cabinets.

▶ Cabinetry made to look like freestanding pieces—like this built-in hutch with shelves, plate rack and drawers—offers a nice contrast when mixed with traditional cabinetry. The mesh details on the cabinetry echo the old-fashioned appeal of the hutch.

compartments of various shapes and sizes within some drawers. Regardless of the outer wood you've chosen for your cabinet face, the inner boxes are generally made of plywood or particleboard. What you want to watch for are tongue-and-groove joints, which promise a long life for the product; glued or stapled joinery can be inferior. In the case of drawers, make sure the boxes are dovetailed to the fronts. Test the drawers; they should glide smoothly. The cabinet door's interior should be free of exposed rough edges.

Inspect your cabinets closely before you have them installed. You'll want to make sure that doors and drawers are solidly constructed and open easily. Check the thickness of the shelves and sides of the cabinet boxes—$\frac{3}{4}$ inch is standard—and make sure the box is square in construction. Look for concealed hinges that don't bend and seams and joint connections that are tight. Finally, make sure the material is consistent; less uniformity is only acceptable in woods such as hickory or cherry, where the grain varies naturally.

▼ In an open plan, cabinetry must perform the dual role of providing plenty of specialized storage and acting as an architectural element that links the kitchen to adjacent living spaces.

Refinishing vs. Refacing

If you're remodeling an older kitchen, but don't need to change cabinet placement, an easy, money-saving option is to update older cabinets either by refinishing or refacing them. Here's the difference between the two methods:

REFINISHING: Cabinets are stripped, then stained and sealed or painted with a washable, scratch-resistant finish. Average cost is between $1,500 and $2,000.

REFACING: Instead of ripping out cabinetry, only doors and drawer fronts are replaced. A new veneer, which may be wood or plastic laminate, is attached to the existing cabinet frames. The hardware and moldings can also be changed to further enhance the new look. Average cost is between $3,000 and $4,000. Obviously, refacing costs less for kitchens with fewer cabinets.

▲ Finishing touches such as deep moldings on the upper cabinets, scrolled brackets supporting the range hood and wood trim that ties the upper cabinets to the lower units are architectural details that enhance a kitchen design.

▲ With a look that's evocative of Scandinavian modern, the cabinets in this kitchen add the only real color in the room. The warm honey glow and fine ridged detailing lend balance to the expanses of cool, smooth stainless steel.

finishing touches

◄ Simple, elegant pewter knobs are in keeping with the classic styling on this kitchen's cabinetry. They complement rather than compete with the carved wood detail.

▲ The homeowner's attention to detail is very evident in this kitchen. Mixing both knobs and drawer pulls provides a way to add another element of interest to cabinetry.

One of the easiest ways to update the look of your kitchen is by replacing cabinet knobs and pulls. Whether you choose sleek metal pulls or antique drawer handles, hardware adds the finishing touch to cabinets and offers a chance to make a strong personal style statement.

Beyond their aesthetic appeal, knobs, handles and drawer pulls must be functional. Choose those that are easy to grasp and simple to clean. Consider round or smooth designs over sharp or angular designs, since it's easy to bump into cabinets when there's more than one cook in the kitchen.

Before you trek to the store, figure out how many knobs and pulls you'll need. Next, take careful measurements to ensure your selections will work on the existing cabinets. When shopping, bring a sample of your old hardware with you to compare sizes and shapes.

Like adding a piece of jewelry to a favorite outfit, knobs and pulls really dress up a kitchen.

▶ Cabinet hardware is only limited by your imagination. Everything from ceramic knobs that echo tile design to clear glass or metals forged into fanciful shapes is available.

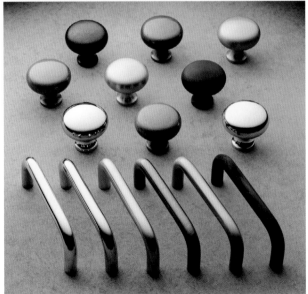

◀ Radiant Capri limestone, a limestone look-alike, is made of 93% quartz.

stunning surfaces

▲ Practical vinyl tile can be chic, too. Styles such as this metallic silver and lead combination complement stainless steel and retro styling.

Surfaces, including floors, walls and countertops, serve as the background on your kitchen's blank canvas. How you choose to "paint" the scene sets the mood for your kitchen. The warmth of apricot color-washed walls that evoke aged Tuscan plaster, the gleam of granite and its cool-to-the-touch feeling on counters or the comfort of wood underfoot can all add a distinctive feeling to a kitchen. It's the sum of these elements that, more than any large appliance or expanse of cabinetry, makes a huge impact on the space itself. Determine the styles, colors and finishes that both excite you and suit your needs—and your budget—best.

Another priority is keeping surfaces clean. Walls and floors should be easy to clean in the high-use areas where splatters and spills are common. Dining areas or work surfaces removed from the cooking area offer you the opportunity to choose style over practical concerns. Some wall spaces can be both highly functional and artistic, such as mosaic backsplashes or tile murals between cabinets and counters or beneath a range hood.

Most of all, when making decisions about these three surfaces, be sure that your choices relate to and complement each other as well as the other key components of a kitchen—cabinetry, appliances and lighting.

countertops

▲ Smart and sleek, a stainless-steel counter is a proven germ fighter that adds to a kitchen's sparkle.

▲ Stainless-steel shelves that match the counters provide convenience and style. The matching cabinet doors and drawer fronts complete the sleek look.

Kitchen countertops are more than just surface workhorses. A kitchen counter serves as the palette for creating memorable meals, even culinary masterpieces, so it must be pleasing to the cook of the house. Counters are also the kitchen's most tactile surface, so they must also be pleasing to the touch. Choosing a surface that's stylish, durable and easy to clean are some of the main things to consider; fortunately there are lots of options that can easily fit the bill.

Stainless Steel

Once the exclusive domain of commercial kitchen designers, stainless steel is now a mainstay in residential kitchens, too. Super-strong, hygienic, water- and heat-resistant, stainless steel has long been considered an ideal surface for food preparation. Comparable in cost to granite and solid-surface materials, stainless has evolved into a contemporary neutral surface, versatile enough to be paired with other materials, such as warm wood or hand-painted tile.

Stone

For timeless beauty and appeal, relatively little maintenance, durability and a lifetime guarantee, it's hard to beat a stone countertop. A natural material that gives kitchens a rich appearance like no other surface can, stone is elegant yet eminently functional and available in a wide variety of choices.

Granite. Available in an array of colors, including blacks, golds, blues, greens and grays, granite costs at least $50 per square foot to upwards of

$100. The type of granite chosen and options like edge treatments can increase the price. Extremely hard and both heat- and stain-resistant, granite can be finished with either a polished or matte surface.

Marble. Softer than granite, marble is susceptible to scratching. Even a dropped pan can cause marble to chip, so it's more suitable for low-use areas of the kitchen. A smaller island or counter section topped with marble is perfect as a baking center. Marble

▲ Rustic yet sophisticated, slate is a great counter alternative to more traditional stone options.

▲ Soapstone counters like this one mellow and darken with age.

▲ Made of 93% quartz, this engineered-stone countertop gets its radiance from crystals. The material is extremely hard, yet it can be cut to fit any space.

Stone—with a Twist

Engineered stone, a popular choice in Europe for about 20 years, is gaining ground here in the States. Composed primarily of bits of stone—usually quartz, but sometimes marble—bound together with an adhesive, engineered stone performs better than real stone in a number of ways. Exceptionally resistant to scratches, burns and stains, engineered stone is also completely nonporous, so it requires no sealing or special cleansers. Engineered-stone countertops are also noteworthy for their appearance. Available in a range of colors, from stone-like neutrals to brilliant reds and blues, engineered-stone countertops literally glitter. The flecks of quartz or marble in them give the material an unparalleled depth and richness, often replicating the look of granite.

comes in a range of colors and patterns. Varieties with less veining and a more uniform appearance tend to cost more. Generally, marble costs slightly less than granite, starting at around $40 per square foot.

Soapstone. Though softer than other stone, soapstone is more resistant to staining. Composed primarily of talc, soapstone has a particularly smooth surface and is available in colors ranging from blue to gray. Soapstone should be sealed periodically with mineral oil; it darkens naturally—and beautifully—over time. Expect to pay about $55 per square foot.

Limestone. Soft and mellow in appearance, limestone is available in whites, yellows, browns, grays and blacks. Naturally more porous than other stone, it requires regular sealing to prevent staining. Less dense varieties scratch more readily than others. Prices average about $50 per square foot.

Slate. Appealing to homeowners with rustic tastes because of its matte surface and irregular split face, slate comes in vivid hues like purples, reds, greens and grays. Although a slate countertop can scratch, sanding with steel wool will remove scratches. Prices start at about $60 or $70 per square foot.

Concrete

Concrete offers an alternative to the polished gleam of granite and marble or the often sterile appearance of synthetic countertops. Precast concrete countertops are created using a template based on countertop measurements. For strength and durability, galvanized wire mesh serves as the countertop's skeleton. The surface is sanded smooth and sealed with a penetrating concrete sealer. A plywood substance is fastened to the floor cabinets to protect them. Concrete countertops can cost more than granite/marble or solid surfacing, sometimes as much as twice the price.

▼ Strong, stain-resistant and scratch-resistant describe Silestone quartz surfacing, which offers options such as a seamless stainless-steel basin for easy cleanup.

▲ A curved breakfast bar affords a spot for quick meals on the go as well as a place to hang out while having a snack. Quartz surfacing works well and looks great in this kitchen's relaxed, comfortable atmosphere.

▲ Crafted in molds, concrete can be fashioned into most any shape. The tri-level counter here provides good looks and performance.

▲ Concrete countertops, like this olive one, are usually formed from Portland-type cement with pigments added for color. These counters can be cast in place or off-site.

▲ Concrete counters can crack over time, so they should be sealed periodically.

▲ A high-style design constructed of Corian offers a sophisticated look.

Laminate

Affordable and practical, high-pressure laminates have been around for decades. Adding to their appeal as great counter surfaces, laminates are now enhanced by new printing technology that allows for nature-inspired patterns that replicate the look of stone and three-dimensional details that give the surface subtle variations. Priced less than stone but similar in appearance, laminates never need sealing. They are, however, susceptible to scorches, scratches and nicks. Expect to pay between $12 and $25 per square foot installed.

Solid Surfacing

Countless design options, easy cleanup and trouble-free maintenance make solid surfacing an attractive choice. Generally crafted out of plastic resins bound by adhesives, solid surfacing has mineral fillers that add color and flame resistance. The resulting "solid" block of material is durable and nonporous. Solid-surfacing manufacturers include Corian, Avonite and Swanstone. Solid surfacing can be cut, drilled and routed like wood. It can withstand moderate—but not extreme—heat without burning. Custom creations, such as a drainboard carved into a countertop

▼ More than one color can be used in solid-surface countertops, which creates myriad custom edging possibilities.

▲ Corian comes in a wide palette of colors, including solids and granite-like styles with tiny flecks of colors.

next to a sink, are possible with solid surfacing. Expect to spend $50 to $100 or more installed.

Wood

Scratches and scorches in wood countertops can be sanded out. But wood is susceptible to water damage, making it a tricky counter choice. Wood counters are best used in cool, dry areas—like a center island counter. Periodic applications of food-grade mineral spirits are necessary to seal the surface. Prices for standard 1-inch maple counters start at about $50 per square foot installed; costs for exotic hardwoods are higher.

▲ Made to look like granite, this sleek Formica surface is durable, yet sports a chic beveled edge that complements this elegant, mahogany-colored cabinetry.

▲ Staron solid surfacing offers custom details that stone can't, such as this convenient, built-in pot rest.

▲ With its warm and natural look, real wood can be a stunning surface. Wood countertops are custom built from hand-selected woods like antique heart pine, iroko, tigerwood or teak, then treated with a waterproof finish.

▲ The classic look of a wood-plank kitchen floor never goes out of style.

▲ Beautiful, durable and naturally abundant, bamboo flooring can be a striking alternative to hardwood.

When it comes to kitchens, floors take a beating. From dropped pots and spilled water to heavy traffic, kitchen floors have to take it all. And they have to last as long as the other kitchen components and continue to look their best.

Fortunately, many of today's flooring options are more than up to the challenge. Although each flooring material has its own distinct appearance and advantages, some materials can be used in conjunction with others to produce one-of-a-kind results. Beyond function, flooring, by virtue of the amount of space it can take up, makes a big design statement. Here is a rundown of the most popular flooring choices.

Wood

Warm, resilient and definitely classic, wood is becoming an increasingly popular choice for kitchen floors. Wood flooring complements wood tones in cabinetry and creates a seamless look from room to room. Wood floors also require regular attention, but quality solid hardwood sealed with polyurethane can stand up to most other flooring options.

Oak and maple are popular wood floor choices, but many of today's kitchens feature exotic woods. Teak from India and Burma, cherry and Santos mahogany from Latin America and kambala and afzelia from Africa all feature rich natural colorations and distinctive grains. Sure they're a bit pricey, but these exotics lessen demand on more popular varieties and create a look that's not as common. Recycled, or "used" wood, is also being installed more often because of its antique beauty and unique appearance. Aged wood reflects intricate grain patterns and timeworn patinas that cannot be duplicated. The fact that recycled wood has a one-of-a-kind history as well as an ecological benefit resonates for many, who enjoy having wood from old barns, warehouses and even ships transformed into magnificent flooring. Another popular addition to wood floors is the use of wood inset borders or centerpiece medallions. This creates a statement on floors akin to tile mosaics on walls.

▲ These 12-inch by 12-inch polished granite floor tiles feature contrasting diamond insets.

▲ This floor, made of solid birch planks, lends a warm, homey feeling to the kitchen.

▲ The addition of smaller mosaic tiles adds interest as a floor tile border.

Cork

As more people recognize its natural advantages, cork is making an inspired comeback. Cushiony to step on yet superbly strong, this unique wood by-product acts as both a thermal insulator and sound absorber. It is also moisture resistant, which makes it an ideal choice for kitchen floors. An added plus is its resilient and elastic nature, which makes it a forgiving work surface for your feet.

Manufactured by grinding up tree bark into small pieces that are then coated with a nontoxic resin binder, cork is an earth-friendly choice since peeled bark grows back within nine years. A finished cork floor retains a smooth, pebbled appearance that is both durable and easy to clean. It also is available in a wide array of colors, including honey, green, brown and ruby, and can be easily stained or stenciled to create a unique look.

Stone and Tile

Stone and tile are the ultimate in texture and style for floors. When it comes to tile, many manufacturers offer coordinating wall/floor tile collections that encourage the use of accent tiles and allow for creative focal points inside the floor space. A move toward using larger-sized tiles, ranging anywhere from 16 to 24 inches, is popular in both compact and expansive spaces. As an alternative to a floor fashioned exclusively in stone, ceramic and stone tiles are often teamed to produce a high-end effect at an affordable price. Porcelain ceramic tiles that resemble natural marble, travertine and Jerusalem stone are also available.

Though durable and easy to maintain, ceramic tile can be hard on legs and feet and slippery. Tile is also slippery when wet, unless a textured tile is chosen. Stone, which may not be the

▼ Although it looks like wood, high-pressure laminate flooring can mimic different plank designs as well as tile floor looks.

most comfortable surface to stand on for extended periods, can also be noisy. If you love the look and are willing to accept a few drawbacks, both stone and tile make a very strong, individual style statement from rustic to elegant. And both can virtually last forever.

Laminate

Laminate floors continually surprise in their ability to mimic their natural counterparts, particularly hardwood, ceramic tile and natural stone. Of late, advancements have allowed beauty to enhance this functional product, producing a floor-covering fabrication that

▲ Another fool-your-eye laminate, made to look like rustic wood planks in a historic home, easily fits together as interlocking flooring.

▲ Sheet vinyl, shown here, is attractive and easy to care for. It's also gentler on your feet, your back and any dropped crockery than other flooring options.

▲ Vinyl is versatile, allowing for decorative details, such as the diamond pattern accents on this white vinyl floor that pick up the bold kitchen wall color.

is expected to grow in popularity. A practical and natural-looking floor surface with endless design possibilities, laminate possesses an intensity of detail in faux wood and stone patterns and the advantage of a change in scale toward wider planks of wood and larger-sized stone and tile. Innovative advances have made installation easier than ever, too.

Vinyl

Besides being durable and beautiful, today's vinyl sheet flooring is surprisingly difficult to distinguish from its hard-surface lookalikes. Do-it-your-selfers who experienced the peel-and-stick variety of vinyl tiles will be pleased to learn that styles are continually progressing to express more natural looks. Following contemporary design trends, vinyl flooring bears a striking resemblance to uniquely textured and weathered woods. The addition of particles to create the appearance of minerals, metal or tiny crystal granules is also used to effectively replicate the look of natural stone.

Linoleum

Everything old is new again, and that goes for linoleum, which is back in vogue as a flooring option, especially in kitchens. Manufactured from linseed oil and other natural components, linoleum is a durable sheet-and-tile flooring. Linoleum has the appeal of a renewable resource, which has helped with its resurgence in popularity. In addition to being durable, it emits no harmful pollutants. Linoleum's expansive color palette, with its host of multicolored designs and marbled effects—as well as classic, bold and colorful border designs—offers unlimited design possibilities.

Concrete

Concrete is not just for driveways anymore. In fact, it's one of today's pricier options in kitchen flooring. Thanks to its durability and understated beauty, low-maintenance concrete flooring has a fresh appeal. A concrete floor can be poured directly onto a properly reinforced subfloor, or it can be installed

▼ Extending flooring out from your kitchen into the adjacent areas, such as hallways, mudrooms or family rooms, gives spaces continuity.

over an existing floor in the form of concrete tiles. You can finds tiles in virtually any size or shape.

Concrete is not cement, although it contains cement, which is a fine gray powder. Add sand and/or rock, plus water and a few lesser additives, and you have concrete. No two tiles are identical, since they are often hand-made. Their appearance on the floor is one-of-a-kind—the perfect solution for kitchen renovators who eschew predictable patterns of mass-produced flooring products.

Color is key, too, since a dye, usually in powder form, is mixed into the concrete before water is added. Infusing concrete with color can turn the drab gray standby into vivid flooring evocative of a Tuscan farmhouse or a Southwestern adobe.

With the right finish, a concrete-tile floor can almost be indistinguishable from a more expensive, marble-tile floor. Concrete also offers the option of personalization by pressing stones, shells or smooth glass "rocks" into the floor before it hardens to create durable, appealing mosaics. Colors, grids or patterns can also be etched into concrete for a custom look.

A concrete-tile floor should cost about three to four times more than a typical linoleum floor. Its handmade appearance and unique texture are earthy and organic. The hairline cracks that sometimes appear in the concrete add to its look without compromising structural integrity. With proper care, these floors can last a lifetime.

▲ A far cry from your mom's linoleum, this vibrant blue-and-yellow checkerboard floor brings up-to-date flavor to a kitchen.

▲ Floors and counters graced with concrete offer a soothing, seamless appearance. Here the material acts as a terrific neutral partner to bright blue cabinets.

walls

▲ Wallpaper with a cheery flower print coupled with a sunny border complements this kitchen's overall country charm.

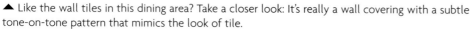

▲ Like the wall tiles in this dining area? Take a closer look: It's really a wall covering with a subtle tone-on-tone pattern that mimics the look of tile.

Nothing personalizes a kitchen more than what graces its walls. Less utilitarian than other parts of the kitchen, the walls let you infuse the space with character, color, even humor. Whether you choose paint, wallpaper or tile, a nod to practicality is key, since walls near cooking and prep areas should be easy to clean. Looking at each wall as a separate unit will allow you to blend decorative wallpaper or beadboard paneling with stainless steel or tile for a look that's all your own.

Wallpaper

The wide variety of available colors, patterns and finishes makes today's wallpaper suitable to any style—from simple and sweet to sleek and chic. Wallpaper or wall coverings are easier to use in kitchens than ever before, thanks to the advent of washable vinyl wallpapers made especially for high-use areas. Vinyl paper is sturdy enough to withstand humidity, heat and temperature changes. Within the category, washable, strippable, scrubbable and colorfast papers all ease the burden of keeping kitchen walls clean.

Choosing a pattern is as easy as taking inspiration from things you love. A favorite platter, a china pattern or a window treatment can all offer ideas. Popular choices include geometric patterns, plaids and stripes or subtle tone-on-tone patterns. Large prints make an oversized room appear smaller and more intimate; a smaller repeat adds visual interest and background color to open up cramped rooms or tiny spaces.

Paint

No matter what the space, color creates a certain ambiance and influences moods. The warm shades on the color wheel—reds, oranges and yellows—give rooms a welcoming energy and can even stimulate the appetite. These shades are just one popular option when it comes to painting a kitchen.

Determining how you want the space to feel when its painted can help you decide how to choose color and when to balance it with neutrals—tans, grays, whites and black. This will provide the room with much needed "breathing space" and add depth and

▲ Graphic paint techniques, such as the blocks of color shown here, are one of the most modern ways to personalize painted walls.

▲ Delicate prints are classic. Inspired by a New England fishing village, this toile evokes a fresh look.

▲ A backsplash can make a glamorous statement. This one combines several types of marble and the use of border tiles to create a three-dimensional effect.

richness. For kitchens that feature neutrals in the form of cabinetry (medium wood tones) or counters (white solid surfacing), a bold color can be a terrific addition to walls.

When choosing paint colors, compare three to five paint chip samples within a color family. Observe the sample chips at different times of day, using natural and artificial light sources. After narrowing down the choices, sample paint by purchasing a pint of each color and painting a small section of the wall in each of the colors. (Some manufacturers offer a small container of a color you'd like to sample at no charge.) Seeing the actual color in the room gives you a better preview of how the finished wall will look.

If you can't find the color you are looking for, many paint manufacturers offer a computerized color-matching process that can match any sample color, whether it's a favorite shirt or a piece of fruit. Last but not least, consider choosing a finish that is washable, such as a semigloss, to prevent the need for constant touch-ups.

Tile

Adding tile to kitchen walls is a beautiful way to enhance a space. If installed properly, kitchen tiles should require little if any upkeep. But this can also be a costly option as tiles can add up, especially if you go beyond ceramic tile and select handcrafted artisan tiles or tumbled marble.

While some elaborate kitchens feature entire walls of tile, even a small addition of tiling along the backsplash or over the cooktop area can make a big impact. Because it reflects light, mirrored tile can be used to brighten a darker kitchen or to make the most of a smaller space. For an artistic centerpiece, try adding tile murals, mosaics or three-dimensional sculpted tiles.

▼ Surrounded by cabinetry resembling a fireplace mantel, this backsplash with an inset border makes a grand impact.

Any of these will dress up a simple kitchen and enhance kitchens with elegant cabinetry and countertops.

Mosaic tiles can be placed individually to create borders. Another option is preformed mosaic designs that are attached to a mesh backing and then applied to walls in one piece.

A popular option for entire walls is the use of subway tiles, the rectangular tiles that were used in many older kitchens and baths. The great benefit of using tile lies with its possibilities. More than any other wall surface for kitchens, tile offers the opportunity to create a one-of-a-kind look.

▲ This tiled wall with a recessed nook features tiles with both glass and metal pigments.

▲ Whether it's citrus fruits or a cornucopia of vegetables, the addition of sporadic painted tiles gives walls an artistic edge.

▲ Creating the appearance of stone, this ceramic tile, set on a diagonal to add interest, pairs perfectly with the stainless-steel range.

◀ This 48-inch dual-fuel range maintains a sleek look with a hidden electronic control panel.

appliance
guide

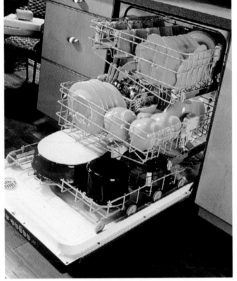

▲ Great new designs in dishwashers offer more space and convenience.

Appliances are the nerve center of any kitchen. In fact, the stove, refrigerator and dishwasher are the true workhorses of the home, handling all the tedious tasks associated with preparing meals.

Today's appliances can turn cooking into a fine art. They also make food preparation fun and cleanup easy. Some make life's everyday jobs easier, others provide convenient perks, but the sum of appliances included in a kitchen is what determines the room's overall functionality.

Style is just as important as function when choosing appliances. Appliances make a big impact in a kitchen by virtue of their number and size. They can be showcased as the powerhouses they are, drawing attention by making a bold, shiny, high-tech statement. Alternately, they can virtually disappear from a space, artfully disguised behind the cover of carefully crafted built-in cabinetry.

Creating a look in which these working elements complement each other, as well as the surrounding cabinetry and counters, makes for a kitchen that's not only efficient but pleasurable to work and dine in. With exterior finishes, from stainless steel and brushed chrome to white, biscuit and black, appliances can be integrated into any kitchen decor—be it Old World, country chic or contemporary.

ranges

▲ This large-capacity double oven offers the versatility of combination cooking modes.

▲ In addition to offering professional-style power, this range is also self-cleaning.

Gas or electric, separate cooktop or traditional range, four or six burners? When it comes to how you want to cook, the questions that inevitably crop up require serious consideration. From double ovens to dual fuel, there are many available models and options that will help get your kitchen cooking.

The most traditional choice, a range, encompasses an oven with a cooktop. Fueled either by electric or gas power, ranges fall into three categories: free-standing, slide-in and drop-in. The most conventional choice, freestanding ranges sit directly on the floor and are the easiest to install and move. Slide-in ranges are a variation on freestanding units, but feature unfinished sides because they are permanently installed between two base cabinets. Drop-in models fit into a counter or island and are supported by a base cabinet built onto the floor. The type of range you choose will depend on whether you are renovating your kitchen or just replac-ing an existing appliance and whether you have gas service in your area.

Beyond the basic choices, today's ranges offer many additional options. Your cooking style can help narrow the field. Chefs who want the ability to cook multiple dishes at once may opt for a commercial-style gas range with six burners. Bakers favor appliances with either a convection oven or an electric oven. Families that eat in shifts will like a range with a warming draw-er to keep plates hot for second sittings.

Gas vs. Electric

Depending on where you live, a gas appliance may be the least expensive to use though it typically costs more to buy. Gas delivers immediate temperature control, responds quickly when adjusting temperatures and has a visible flame that lets you see the heat level. Unlike gas cooktops, electric burners respond more slowly to temperature adjustments, and the burners cannot cool down or heat up in an instant. However, electric ovens pro-

▲ Additional features like the lift-up vent on this five-burner cooktop give home cooks plenty of options to consider during the selection process.

▲ A sleek appearance, easy cleanup and added surface space are some of the advantages to an electric cooktop.

▲ An oven with a warming drawer keeps prepared dishes piping hot until dinner is served—a must-have for cooks who entertain.

vide consistent heat for better baking and even broiling.

Dual-fuel ranges offer the best of both worlds, combining an electric oven with a gas cooktop. Dual-fuel ranges are a must for cooks who enjoy being able to adjust heat simply by looking at a gas flame, but also want the self-cleaning and baking advantages of an electric oven.

Cooktops

The cooktop is another factor to consider. Most ranges have four to six cooking elements of different sizes to accommodate a variety of cookware.

Electric ranges have come a long way from conventional coil elements. Ceramic glass models feature heating elements under a smooth top. Models with quick-heating quartz-halogen and induction elements offer precise cooking temperatures.

Gas ranges use burner grids to suspend cookware over the heat. Models with sealed gas burners contain spills, allowing for easy cleanup.

Both types of ranges can feature special warming zones to hold prepared dishes until the entire meal is ready to be served. They can also include adaptable bridge burners that expand the

cooktop's heating zone to accommodate oversized pots or roasting pans, and simmer settings to keep constant, low temperatures for even heating.

Solo cooktops, those that are installed separate from ovens, typically come in widths ranging from 27 to 36 inches. They are available with two to six burners, and can be installed in a counter below cabinetry, in a peninsula or in an island.

A separate oven (installed in a cabinet or wall) is an essential companion to the cooktop. It can also be used to supplement an existing range. Most models are 24, 27 or 30 inches wide.

▼ Superior performance can be achieved with this 60-inch range, which features convection baking and infrared oven broilers for restaurant-quality results. You can also customize with the optional griddle or charbroiler.

▲ Big breakfasts and family feasts are easy when two cooks can work together side-by-side. This 60-inch dual-fuel range, complete with griddle top, is an ideal choice.

▲ A dual-fuel slide-in range offers high-tech performance in standard range size.

▲ This five-burner, 36-inch cooktop is ideal for island installation. It features porcelain-coated cast-iron grates and a tempered glass surface with front and center controls.

▲ Double ovens don't necessarily need to be stacked above each other. The two shown here—across the aisle from one another—allow two cooks unobstructed access. Installed at a height several inches above the floor, they also create a prominent design element.

Single or double wall ovens are a popular option as either the kitchen's main oven or as additional ovens.

Getting just the right degree of heat is easier with gas and electric cooktops that have variable heat burners. A popular configuration includes two high-powered burners for stir-frying and searing meats, one low-powered burner for simmering delicate sauces, and a standard burner—ideal for the rigors of everyday cooking.

Another helpful addition is the bridge burner, which heats the area between two round burners, creating an evenly heated surface for griddles or oblong pans that eliminates cold spots.

Hoods

Without proper ventilation, cooking can create odors and grime that accumulate on walls and appliances and pollute the air. A range hood with an updraft system is not only the most effective way to clear the air, it's also the required choice for today's powerful professional-style ranges.

Cooking surfaces should have adequate ventilation, in the form of a hood powered at least 150 CFM (cubic feet per minute), vented to the outdoors. Beyond that basic requirement, sound is another consideration when choosing a range hood. Quieter range hoods are available that do the work of clean-

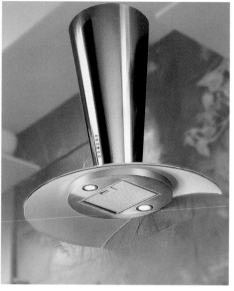

▲ This range hood is crafted of cylindrical stainless steel with an oval handblown glass canopy. Ultrasleek and ultracontemporary, it pairs 21st century design with up-to-the-minute technology, including six fan speeds and touch-pad controls.

◀ A sleek, smart profile gives this efficient hood a chic European look.

ing the air without adding noise pollution. Matching the power of a hood to the power of a range ensures you'll get the efficiency you expect. For instance, a professional-style range with an output of 90,000 BTUs would require 900 CFM of ventilation.

A downdraft system offers a less powerful but subtle alternative to a prominent hood. Air is exhausted to the outside through vents built into the cooktop, or a vent is built into a cabinet behind the cooktop, popping up at the push of a button when needed. But be warned that steam from taller pots and pans may escape its pull, as can anything that's too far from the vent.

▲ A 36-inch-wide professional chimney hood is a perfect match for pro-style cooktops.

▲ Besides cleaning the air, this hood offers halogen lights for extra illumination.

▲ An arched face gives this hardworking hood softer curve appeal.

▲ A roomy 2-cubic-foot microwave paired with a 30-inch single wall oven creates high style and functionality.

▲ Over-the-range microwaves are available with a wide array of features, including convection cooking.

Offering the ultimate cooking shortcut, microwave ovens are essential equipment. Speeding defrosting and allowing for instant reheating, melting and more, microwaves have been redefined. Appliances that feature safe, fast and reliable performance and a more compact design have replaced their bulky predecessors.

Combination microwave/convection ovens bring together dual cooking methods to deliver meals that can be browned, roasted or crisped in record time. Though they're more expensive than either solo microwave or convection ovens, combination ovens bring the best features of both types to one unit. Different models work in different ways, but most allow either microwave or convection cooking separately, or a combination of both at once. More advanced models offer special cooking cycles that allow you to program a period of microwave cooking, then a browning or crisping period with convection cooking.

Size Matters

Microwaves are available in three classes: compact (less than 0.8 cubic feet), midsize (0.8 to 1.1 cubic feet) and full-size (1.2+ cubic feet). The measurement refers to the interior size of the oven (including corner areas) rather than the outside dimension. The size of the microwave often determines its power—compact ovens range from 400 to 700 watts, midsize ovens from 600 to 800 watts and full-size from 650 to more than 1,000 watts. Many microwaves in all sizes offer varying power levels—four or five are adequate—for different kinds of cooking.

Both countertop and over-the-range versions abound with options. Since microwaves are emitted in a fixed pattern, most ovens feature a turntable that keeps food moving to assure more even heating.

Convection ovens are available in 24- and 30-inch widths and may be either gas or electric. Convection ovens demand much lower heat settings than conventional ovens because heated air is circulated constantly over dishes. Therefore, using a convection oven can realize a 25- to 30-percent reduction in cooking temperatures and a 20- to 60-percent reduction in cooking time over conventional ovens. Many models offer optional power levels, including a gentle bake cycle ideal for delicate pastries and meringues.

▲ In addition to slashing cooking time, this 900-watt microwave oven offers a space-saving two-slice toaster.

▲ This over-the-counter carousel microwave includes a sensor to make cooking easier. It's also a great space saver.

Special Features

Top-of-the-line microwaves include sensors that will either shut down the cooking cycle or switch to a warming cycle when the food is done. The more advanced sensors are infrared and check the surface temperatures of the food being cooked. Though they are less common, some microwaves even include moisture sensors that stop the cooking cycle before food begins to dry out.

▲ An over-the-stove microwave affords the convenience of easy transfer during food prep.

refrigerators

▲ Outfitted with a sliding, full-width shelf, a freezer drawer offers two levels of storage for easy organizing.

▲ A commercial-style side-by-side unit in stainless steel stands out with its sleek handles.

Refrigeration has come a long way since Grandma's icebox. Modern refrigerators do so much more than simply store perishable foods. They can actually adapt to your family's lifestyle and to your preference for food storage. Today's models can even blend seamlessly with your cabinetry, rendering those once behemoth boxes virtually invisible.

The two most popular refrigerator styles are side-by-side and top-bottom models, which usually have the freezer on top. Many manufacturers also offer the latter style with the refrigerator on top of a lower pull-out freezer drawer—a smart idea since we're in the refrigerator more often than the freezer, so its contents should be at eye level.

Built-in refrigerators are designed to transition perfectly from kitchen cabinetry, staying flush with a 24-inch-deep countertop. These built-in models can feature stainless-steel doors or accommodate an overlay of your cabinetry finish and hardware.

Cool features

A typical family might open the doors to a refrigerator some 60 times a day, so choosing the best model for your needs is crucial. When shopping look for:

Smart shelves. Large containers or tall bottles should fit on shelves as is or with easy adjustments.

Easy access. You need to get to the contents of the refrigerator easily. Consider roll-out shelves and clear drawers and bins that allow you to see what's inside without opening them.

Strong seal. Doors that require a good tug to open have a solid seal, a must for keeping food cold and preventing spoilage.

Simple cleaning. Drawers and door compartments should be removable; shelves should have raised edges to help control spills.

Crisper feature. Crisper bins should be humidity controlled to keep produce fresh.

In addition to basic white, beige and black finishes, many manufacturers offer custom paneling options as well as stainless steel. Customizing your new refrigerator's interior is also possible, at

▲ Designed like an armoire, this refrigerator offers side-by-side door styling on top and a convenient bottom pull-out freezer.

▲ This 42-inch built-in improves storage capabilities with wide shelving that is easily adjusted to a desired height.

▲ Good looks meet good sense with this stainless-steel refrigerator. Its sleek design includes a freezer on the top with the Smart Water filtration system.

additional cost. Choose from an assortment of pull-out shelves and bins, racks and tilt-out storage drawers, plus adjustable humidity crispers to control moisture and temperature for different foods. Other conveniences include condiment carousels and a hanging bottle rack for chilling wine.

If you entertain frequently, a refrigerator with the capacity to make large amounts of ice in a short amount of time is essential. A quick-chill shelf, which can be used to cool a bottle of wine in a fraction of the typical time,

can also prove useful. Some refrigerators offer a family-friendly feature called a refreshment, or snack, center. Consisting of a small pull-down door, it allows quick access to frequently chosen drinks and snacks, without having to open the entire door.

Another popular option is point-of-use refrigerator drawers that can store fresh vegetables or meats by the sink or range. Wine or beverage coolers, the same size as small refrigerators, fit under counters or in islands, offering easy access for guests.

▲ These refrigerators combine a retro '50s look with 21st century technology. Their rounded corners, chrome wings and hot colors blend with modern conveniences.

▼ A must for oenophiles, an under-the-counter refrigerator/wine chiller holds up to 50 bottles and offers seven horizontal shelves so corks stay moist.

▲ New advances in refrigeration include temperature-controlled compartments and a speed thaw feature.

▲ New 36-inch-wide refrigerators feature added storage space to handle large party platters and oversized foods.

▲ The doors on side-by-side refrigerators keep the food prep area more open than those on a top-bottom unit would.

STYLE NOTES

Water Works

Consider refrigerator models that include in-line water filtration systems. Water is channeled through a replaceable cartridge, providing purer water for cooking, drinking and making ice. Usually a light on the door of the refrigerator (or inside it) indicates when the filter needs to be replaced—about every three months or so. Most refrigerator systems utilize a carbon filter, similar to those used on water-filter pitchers.

▲ A tilted display shelf showcases favorite wines while keeping them properly chilled.

dishwashers

▲ A dishwasher outfitted with a panel that matches the surrounding cabinetry creates a smooth stretch of uninterrupted cabinets.

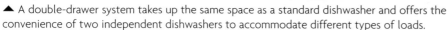
▲ A double-drawer system takes up the same space as a standard dishwasher and offers the convenience of two independent dishwashers to accommodate different types of loads.

The appliance that does the kitchen's dirty work and is put to use day in and day out has become quieter and more efficient over the years. Besides working a lot better than older models (no need to waste time and water on prerinsing), the dishwashers of today look a lot better, too. The proliferation of models with sparkling stainless-steel liners, hidden control panels and attractive hardware has given the image of the dishwasher a transformation worthy of Cinderella.

Most brands of built-in dishwashers come in a standard 24-inch width with two racks. Higher-end models feature electronic controls and other specialty features that increase with price. Dishwashers can be lined with either plastic or porcelain, but the top-end choice is stainless steel, both for its sturdiness and ability to withstand high temperatures.

Although most brands claim to have low-noise machines, "minimized vibration" and "proper insulation" are the buzzwords associated with units that are considerably quieter than others.

You might be surprised at the number of amenities that can factor into dishwasher decision-making. Among them are cubbies and movable baskets for smaller items; adjustable racks that allow for oversized or odd-shaped dishes; a self-cleaning filter and hard-food dispenser, which grinds up food and disposes of it automatically; and a high-temperature cycle that ensures optimum sanitization.

▲ Perfect for a home bar, this dishwasher drawer makes fast work of a load of stemware.

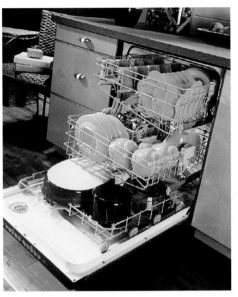

▲ Among the newest advances is a three-rack design that accommodates large dishes. The updated cleaning system scours baked-on grit, saving time, water and energy.

▶ With controls tucked away on top of the door and a full-length frameless design, this dishwasher looks stylish and streamlined in any modern kitchen design.

Other whistles and bells include a time-delay feature that allows you to run the machine on a timer, a dirt sensor that determines how much hot water is needed and specialized cycles for china or pots and pans.

Aesthetically, a hidden control panel (located in the top end of the door) and a flat, uninterrupted front panel create the sleek look that's become a design standard. Integrated panels to match cabinetry or stainless-steel front panels complete the look.

◀ This kitchen divides and conquers by positioning two sinks at separate ends of the kitchen. One is used in conjunction with the dishwasher; the other is perfectly located for food preparation.

fixtures & fittings

Whether we are filling pots for pasta, rinsing produce or washing our hands, we go to our kitchen sink at least 20 times a day. Because this area gets so much use, a sink and faucet combination that not only complements your kitchen but also is highly functional is essential.

Sinks choices abound, but the key factor in decision-making is determining which size, configuration and materials will best fit your situation and budget. A large single-bowl sink is desirable for kitchens that are less than 150 square feet. A double-bowl sink is recommended for larger-size kitchens. Very large kitchens can benefit from an additional small salad/prep sink that includes a disposal.

Mounting Options

Sinks can be mounted in four different ways: surface-mounted, undermounted, countertop-integrated and apron, or farmhouse. Each mounting method has benefits and disadvantages depending on your needs and preferences.

Surface-mounted sinks, the most common type, are relatively inexpensive and easy to install. Some have a self-rimming edge while others need an additional rim (usually metal) to join the sink's edge to the counter surface. The self-rimming styles are easier to keep clean. Sinks can also have a "tile-in" edge that mounts flush with a tiled counter surface for a more appealing appearance.

Undermounted sinks fasten to the underside of countertops with special clips that screw into the top. This sink type requires finishing the edges of the counter opening for the sink and drilling holes into the countertop for the faucets and spout. Undermounted sinks make for easier cleanups, allowing you to sweep crumbs directly into the sink rather than having to negotiate over a rim edge. They also look more elegant and provide a smoother transition from countertop to sink.

Integrated sinks, consisting of one solid piece with a surrounding counter surface, offer a pulled-together look in the kitchen. Since they are part of the countertop, installation is a one-step process. Integrated sinks can be made from acrylics, solid-surface materials and stainless steel.

Apron, or farmhouse, sinks are another popular option. Comprised of one large bowl with an exposed front panel, these sinks mimic the style of sinks found in historic farmhouses or the cottages of the French countryside. Attractive and complementary to many interior styles, these sinks are difficult to incorporate into existing designs, as they require out-of-the-ordinary cabinet specifications.

Materials Matter

After determining a mounting style, choosing a material for your sink comes next. The most common choices are stainless steel, enameled cast iron or steel, solid surface and composite.

Stainless-steel kitchen sinks have a long track record. Stainless doesn't chip, cleans easily and can be molded as part of a stainless-steel countertop to match commercial-style appliances. The best stainless-steel sinks are made

▼ This elegant undermounted sink with copper faucet is situated in a white marble countertop. Located between a heavy-duty ice maker and an under-counter refrigerator, it is a key component of a convenient kitchen wet bar.

of 18-gauge steel or heavier. The only negative associated with stainless sinks is their tendency to show scratches. Over time, stainless does take on a natural patina that can be quite appealing. A quality stainless-steel sink should cost between $350 and $800.

A brightly colored, enameled cast-iron or steel sink is a cheery addition to any kitchen. These types are made by fusing a coating of porcelain to the metal. The cast-iron versions are more costly, but are stronger and tend to be less noisy than steel. Though relatively easy to clean, they tend to chip and can stain. These enameled sinks cost between $300 and $1,500.

Solid-surface sinks have grown in popularity because of the wide choice of colors and designs available. Made from a mixture of mineral compounds and polyester or resin, solid-surface sinks can easily be molded from the same piece as the countertop. Scratches buff out, but these materials can stain easily. Solid-surface sinks also will not tolerate hot pans. Prices range from $300 to $700.

Man-made, composite sinks are formed from quartz compounds combined with acrylic resins. Like solid-surface sinks, they can be an integrated part of a countertop and are available in many styles and colors. However, composite materials are much more heat- and stain-resistant than solid surfacing. Sharp knives should be avoided around this surface as they can leave marks. Most composite sinks are priced between $350 and $500.

▲ Locating the primary sink in an island, rather than against a wall or under a window, allows the person washing dishes to visit easily with guests at the counter.

▲ Made of impact- and stain-resistant material, this composite sink is easy to maintain.

faucet form

▲ Coupled with a deep sink, this high-arching faucet can accommodate bulky pots and pans, as well as tall flower vases.

Like a work of art, a faucet on a kitchen sink can set a tone, add a bit of whimsy or even act as the central design focus in a kitchen setting. Seemingly limitless styles and material choices have transformed these formerly utilitarian objects into architectural centerpieces. And many of the faucet choices offer surprising functionality. For the pure pleasure of dressing up the kitchen sink without exorbitant cost, nothing compares to some of the newest designs in faucets. The many

features included with kitchen faucets also make them as marvelous to use as they are to behold.

Innovations that marry function with form include kitchen faucets with pull-out sprayers incorporated right into the spout and others with highly arched spouts to allow for easy filling of pots or vases. All come in a stunning array of styles from classic to quirky. For the resident gourmet, some lines of kitchen faucets are available that duplicate those found in fine restaurants.

Many time-honored designs have been given updated details for a fresher, more unique look and improved functionality. Some current faucets for kitchens are designed with sensors that detect changes in pressure and temperature when water is being turned on at another faucet in the house. These marvels automatically adjust pressure and temperature to keep them more constant. Others have an anti-scald feature that allows you to set a maximum temperature.

This arched-neck faucet swivels at its base to fill either basin of the double sink. A built-in pump soap dispenser minimizes clutter; a single-flip lever controls water flow and temperature.

Extras! Extras!

For added convenience, consider these sink features to make food preparation even easier:

- Extra-deep bowls for soaking large pots and pans.
- Rear-positioned drains, which offer more bowl space and allow for more under-counter cabinet space.
- Off-center faucets, which allow you to maximize bowl space.
- Sink accessories, such as cutting boards, drain baskets and colanders.

▲ Get a sleek look with this stainless-steel sink with a side sink and ridges for drainage.

▲ Its graceful design and old-time pull crank handle give this faucet an antique appeal.

A Fine Finish

Typically, faucets are formed of either metal or plastic at their bases. The best quality and longest-lasting faucets are made from solid brass; these are also the most expensive. Zinc-alloy bodies are durable and less costly than brass. Plastic varieties are also available. These are inexpensive, but do not perform as well as the metal variety.

Faucet finishes vary from the standard chrome and brass to pewter and nickel. There are also combinations of finishes, such as chrome and brass. Higher-end versions include bisque and ceramic finishes, and fine metal overlays of gold or sterling silver.

There is a rainbow of color choices in ceramic finishes as well as a wide range of metallics—everything from classic polished or satin chrome and brass to brushed copper and nickel with deep bronze and warm, silvery tones. The painted or enamel finishes allow for easy coordinating with kitchen design schemes.

▼ This elegant cast-iron sink is enhanced by a decorative, lace-like pattern.

▲ This cast-iron sink features an ultrasmooth, nonporous enamel surface that repels particles of dirt and bacteria with a simple rinse of water.

▲ A restaurant-quality pot-filler next to the range eliminates the need for carrying a heavy vessel of water from sink to stove.

▲ Both a snap to clean and easy to use, this sleek, double-basin, integrated stainless-steel sink— positioned under a double window—is a beautiful, functional addition.

fine fittings

▲ Taking on dirty pots and pans is easy with this faucet, featuring a 59-inch extractable hose.

Different types of kitchen faucets are distinguished by the way the handles and spouts are arranged. Single-handled faucets are especially convenient in the kitchen. They include a center-set knob or lever above a spout, providing ease of use.

Wide-spread faucets have hot and cold valves and spouts that are mounted separately. When shopping you need to be aware of "centers"—the distance between the center of one handle and the center of another. Kitchen sinks usually have 8-inch centers, but some 6-inch ones can be found. If you are replacing an old faucet, it's best to take it with you to purchase a new one.

In place of washers, most quality faucets employ either a plastic or ceramic cartridge; a plastic, brass or stainless-steel ball valve; or a ceramic disk. The handles and spout may be made of solid brass or plastic. Experts recommend solid brass fittings and a ceramic disk inside for durability and for handling extreme temperatures.

▲ A traditional, stainless-steel sink—complete with white porcelain faucet handles that match the cabinetry hardware—complements this kitchen's classic good looks.

▲ This elegant sink is a perfect choice for a butler's pantry.

▲ High on function and ease of use, this gleaming chrome faucet with single-lever operation is a perfect partner to the deep stainless-steel sink. The design allows for one-handed operation.

◀ These pendant lamps offer the unique design element of a pulley system, allowing for both overall and close-up illumination.

kitchen lighting

▲ Dramatic, vertical wood-clad windows—wood on the inside, fiberglass on the outside—light up a breakfast room.

Good lighting is important in any room, but none as much as the kitchen. More than just a place to cook, the kitchen has become a multiuse space requiring different levels of light. Kitchens require light for making work and prep tasks easier and safer, and for making the space inviting to guests—who always seem to congregate where all the action takes place. Since lighting is needed for both practical reasons and to create a space that radiates warmth and comfort, different kinds of lighting are necessary to create the ideal degree of illumination.

Combining natural light with thoughtful placement of artificial light-ing ensures that a kitchen can be just as enjoyable at dusk as when it's bathed in sunshine. Taking time to consider the natural light you have (in terms of windows and exposures) and how it can be maximized will also dictate the placement of artificial light.

Artificial light can't compete with the beauty and benefits of natural light. Choosing the right windows is essential to capturing the perfect amount of sunlight. Windows that allow the maximum amount of natural light in, while keeping out both winter drafts and the heat of summer, make the difference between a sunny, comfortable kitchen and one that requires constant illumination by artificial means.

◀ Offering elegance and subtle illumination, this dining area chandelier features a dark antiqued-nickel base with silver accents and frosted-glass shades.

▲ Simple, yet classic and versatile, this three-arm Beaux Arts-style chandelier features pendant arms and an antique brass finish.

Sunshine may be the light of choice, but adding more natural light to a kitchen isn't always convenient or even possible. Fortunately, artificial light not only serves to brighten a space and make it more functional, lighting fixtures also bring decorative impact by echoing a kitchen's style.

By choosing the right amount and kinds of lights, you can make a kitchen more inviting, practical and attractive. Make sure lighting is not an afterthought; choose lighting when a new kitchen is in the planning stages. By making it an integral part of your kitchen plan and weighing lighting as important as any other decision, you guarantee all the other elements of your kitchen will be seen in the best light possible.

When lighting a kitchen, forget the all-or-nothing approach. One or two ceiling fixtures in the center of the room cannot be expected to perform all the necessary lighting functions. Lighting designers recommend instead a technique called "layered lighting," which involves using a combination of fixtures to achieve optimum results.

Lighting Basics

Understanding how lighting works in a room starts with knowing the four basic functions of light: accent, ambient, decorative and task. Accent lighting is used to highlight details and objects, such as a decorative backsplash or the tops of cabinets, and usually involves adjustable recessed lights. Ambient

▲ This pendant lamp recreates an industrial-era look with a domed prismatic lampshade, capped bottom and polished nickel fittings.

▲ Gilded iron, alabaster-style glass and a distinctive gold finish are design elements of this kitchen's chandelier and sconces, which combine to create an elegant, well-lit atmosphere.

lighting is a soft, indirect light that makes people feel comfortable and draws them into a space. Hidden lighting on top of a kitchen cabinet and wall sconces are good examples of ambient light. Decorative light adds sparkle to a space and can be as simple as hanging pendants over a kitchen island. Task lighting is used for activities such as cooking or reading. The best task light falls between your head and the work surface. Under-cabinet lights will illuminate a countertop, making meals easier to prepare.

Including a mix of under-cabinet lights, recessed lighting and hanging pendant lights can make a kitchen come to life. Ceiling height, natural light, surface finishes and kitchen layout are all important things to consider when planning lighting for this space. For instance, a kitchen featuring white cabinets and appliances will require less illumination than a kitchen with a dark wood decor.

▲ Pale honey art glass gives these Arts and Crafts-inspired pendants panache. The weathered bronze finish helps complete the look.

natural light

▲ Positioning kitchen windows above the sink ensures that a chef will have a pleasant view while performing mundane tasks.

▼ This foldaway handle that won't disturb window treatments is one of the many advances in window technology.

Windows are your kitchen's visual portals to the outside world. They add character and expression to your home's exterior, while flooding the interior with refreshing, natural light.

Windows can also be expensive and difficult to replace, so choosing kitchen windows wisely is time well spent. Deciding which windows will work best involves a number of factors. Ideally, you want a window that is easy to install, easy to operate and properly insulated. Choose a style that complements the architectural design of your home or, more specifically, the decor of your kitchen.

Window Shopping

Many window styles are available with various features and advantages. There are windows that are fixed, and others that can swing in, out and from the top. Other models slide up, down and sideways (see STYLE NOTES at right for details on window types).

Special features in windows include "self-cleaning" glass, which cuts down on outside window maintenance. The glass features a transparent coating that keeps streaks to a minimum. Decorative glass, often sandwiched between two plain panes, can dress up your home on the inside and out. Retractable screens that are out of sight when not in use are a popular choice for windows that offer great views. Hardware colors and styles range from oil-rubbed bronze to muted pewter.

▲ Casement windows available in a choice of hardwood interiors offer the benefits of new windows with the appeal of Craftsman styling.

▲ Divided-light wood windows lend new spaces a timeless elegance, as well as eye-catching architectural detail.

▲ Create an instant solarium with a variety of floor-to-ceiling windows.

STYLE NOTES

Window Styles

Not sure which windows best suit you? Here's a guide to the various types:

AWNING WINDOWS are hinged at the top and swing out, away from the house. They are usually positioned high on a wall, and often in rows, creating walls of light. Because of their placement, awning windows usually don't require window treatments. This type is suitable for many architectural styles, including Tudor, ranch and contemporary designs.

CASEMENT WINDOWS swing open on side hinges. Casements that crank inward are French style; those that crank outward are considered English. Casements are an energy-efficient choice because when the wind blows, the window closes more tightly. They work well in Tudor, French, English, ranch and contemporary settings.

DOUBLE-HUNG WINDOWS consist of top and bottom portions that operate in a rectangular frame. Both halves can slide up and down and take up no

▲ A combination of casement, fixed and eyebrow windows creates a dramatic kitchen focal point.

inside or outside space. Double-hungs are appropriate in Colonial, Craftsman, Victorian and other traditional designs.

FIXED WINDOWS are decorative in function; they do not open and close. Eyebrow windows and picture windows are common fixed types. Fixed windows fit in with just about every architectural style, depending on the shape of the window.

Framing Options

A window's frame is what holds the sash, glass panes and hardware together. Proper framing is important because it dictates how the new window will look, insulate and function. Vinyl, wood, aluminum, fiberglass and composite windows are the most common types of frames.

Vinyl. Easy-to-maintain, inexpensive and durable, vinyl frames offer plenty of advantages. They are moisture resistant, come in a wide variety of colors and require less maintenance than wood. But despite better installation procedures and advances in technology, some vinyl windows can suffer from thermal expansion. Still, the relatively inexpensive price tag of vinyl windows makes them an attractive option. In some cases, vinyl frames can cost about half as much as same-sized wood frames.

Wood. Classic, warm and rich in texture, wood windows add a lot to a kitchen's appeal. Cherry, pine, oak and mahogany windows let you complement decor by coordinating windows with cabinetry. Wood can be milled into custom designs and shapes, and painted or stained to match the rest of the home. Wood windows also provide excellent protection from outside elements if maintained properly, either through regular painting or staining.

Aluminum. Lightweight yet strong, aluminum offers a good framing option for windows. Available in a wide variety of sizes and shapes, aluminum windows feature an anodized, or baked-on, enamel finish. Aluminum frames are hardy and require less main-

▼ Two banks of double-hung wood windows create walls of light that bathe this kitchen's dining area in brightness.

STYLE NOTES

Save Energy

Energy-efficient windows can cut heating and cooling bills by up to 15 percent. Windows that consist of two layers of glass, called double-glazed, are twice as efficient as single-glazed. Additional energy-friendly window features include a low-emissivity coating, a transparent film that reduces heat loss; a coating that reduces heat and also reflects glare and ultraviolet light; and a window with inert gas—either argon or krypton—that fills the space between the windowpanes to improve energy performance.

▲ The wood screens on these casement windows are virtually invisible, which allows for more breathtaking ocean views. The exterior of the screens are clad in aluminum for added durability.

▲ Swing-out casements, with transoms overhead, offer access to hard-to-clean places.

▲ Windows make an architectural statement in this kitchen. Highly decorative windows are now part of manufacturers' "stock" collections.

tenance than wood, but lesser quality aluminum windows may suffer from heat loss and condensation problems. Aluminum windows cost less than comparable vinyl or wood frames.

Fiberglass. Prized for its strength, fiberglass is an increasingly popular window material. With a sleek look that blends well in modern-style kitchens, fiberglass can be stained or painted. Structurally sound, but heavy in weight, fiberglass doesn't offer the thinness of a vinyl or aluminum frame. Fiberglass costs less than wood but more than vinyl.

Composite. A frame made of two or more materials draws on the individual strengths of each material. Vinyl-clad wood windows combine the strength of wood with the durability and weather resistance of vinyl. The inside wood surfaces can be painted or stained to match the room's interior, while the outside vinyl surface allows for easy maintenance. Aluminum-clad windows have a wood interior and aluminum exterior for a more climate-impervious product. Aluminum-clad wood is strong, durable and available in a range of sizes and colors.

▲ Vinyl windows, available in a variety of dramatic shapes, won't rot, warp or corrode.

▼ An abundance of simple, double-hung windows makes this dining area feel like an extension of the outdoors.

▲ A combination of small fixed panes and larger casement windows reinforces the simple Craftsman styling of this kitchen.

▲ Modern insulated windows in a classic style can suit the architecture of older homes while offering optimum energy efficiency.

▲ This aluminum-clad wood casement window is designed to resist moisture.

▲ Windows with impact-resistant glass provide the toughness needed to weather the elements without sacrificing aesthetic appeal.

MAKING IT HAPPEN

working with professionals

EXPERT TIPS

Finding the Best

To build a list of professionals to interview, solicit word-of-mouth referrals from friends, family and real-estate agents. Also check with these organizations—they provide regional listings of professionals:

Architects: The American Institute of Architects (AIA); www.aiaonline.com.

Interior Designers: The American Society of Interior Designers (ASID); www.interiors.org, or (800) 775-ASID.

Contractors and Remodelers: National Association of the Remodeling Industry (NARI); www.nari.org.

Certified Kitchen Designers: The National Kitchen & Bath Association (NKBA); www.nkba.com, or (800) 843-6522.

Finding and working with the right professionals is one of the most important steps you will take. The design/building team you hire is key to the success of your project. Without reputable and experienced architects, designers, contractors and trades people, you're vulnerable to unreasonable delays, unexpected costs and poor workmanship.

To assemble your team, you'll need to understand the role of each professional and consider any special circumstances regarding your project. For instance, if you live in a historic house, you may want a professional whose expertise is in restoration. If your plans include additions to a space that would expand the footprint of your home, you'll want the expertise of an architect on your team.

If the ease of a one-stop-shop experience is more to your liking, working with an established showroom that can connect you with experts to work on your project might be the solution. The three major professionals that can help make your dream kitchen a reality are a designer (either an interior designer or a certified kitchen designer), an architect and a general contractor.

Finally, before you go any further in planning or actual work, make sure you're adequately insured, or your project could turn out to be a much more expensive proposition.

designers

Even in the hands of an experienced contractor, your kitchen project will require you to make a lot of choices—from a color palette for painted walls and trim to material choices for floor and counter surfaces, even to the placement of light switches. It's easy to watch time (and money) slip away as you try to keep it straight and consider options and specifications. Prevent your project from becoming an all-consuming one with the help of an interior designer.

Working with your architect and contractor to spearhead your remodeling project, a designer can save you time and money and ensure that you get the look and comfort you want from what stands to be a significant investment in your kitchen. An experienced designer will help you avoid the mistakes you might naturally make— and regret later on. With the assistance and expertise of a designer, the end result will be a more functional kitchen and less money spent to rectify errors.

Offering more specialization, a certified kitchen designer (CKD) can often bring a greater level of expertise to kitchen projects. These professionals keep up-to-date on the latest products, materials and technologies, as well as on building and safety codes. If you decide to work with a CKD, you can expect a detailed outline of your project describing every element to be included—from wiring and plumbing to appliances and fixtures to countertops, flooring and cabinetry. For these

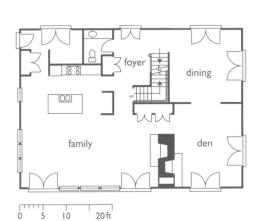

▲ This layout was designed to allow the owners to undertake multiple chores within steps of each other, such as doing laundry, preparing meals and overseeing homework.

▲ Great design ideas and an architect's sensibility are the secrets behind effective kitchens. In this layout, the traffic flows easily to different rooms in the house, and ample storage keeps things organized.

EXPERT TIPS

Peruse Portfolios

When you set up interviews, ask potential designers to bring their portfolios. These most likely will include high-quality photographs and presentation boards with fabric and wall-treatment samples. Studying portfolios will help you figure out which designer's style is most compatible with your taste.

▲ To create a consistent sense of old-fashioned appeal throughout the kitchen, a designer was dispatched to find antique accessories, such as the retro scale.

professionals, comfort, safety and aesthetics are equal considerations in the success of your kitchen project.

A designer's qualifications is an important consideration. Design education may range from a degree from an accredited university to on-the-job training. Ask about their experience and whether they are licensed and/or accredited by any design associations. Ask designers for references, then follow up with phone calls to their clients, ideally both former and current.

All things being equal, cost can greatly influence your final decision. Different designers offer different fee structures. Some take a markup on the materials, furnishings or products they provide. The difference between the designer's cost and what the client pays covers the designer's services. Many others bill for the amount of time worked, with rates ranging from $50 to $125 an hour or more, depending on the area of the country where you live and the designer's availability and

experience. Still others charge a flat fee for a project or use a combination of billing methods.

Regardless of the fee structure, you should know what you'll be expected to pay up front and how and when you will be billed. Find out how you will be apprised of finances as the project progresses and how costs over budget will be handled. If you are satisfied with the answers, the designer should provide a contract that puts all the terms you have agreed upon into writing.

▶ The wall cabinets surrounding this kitchen bar store an array of glasses within easy reach. Because the shelves are adjustable, they can be raised or lowered to accommodate every sort of glass—from champagne flutes to old-fashioneds. That's just smart planning!

[before]

[after]

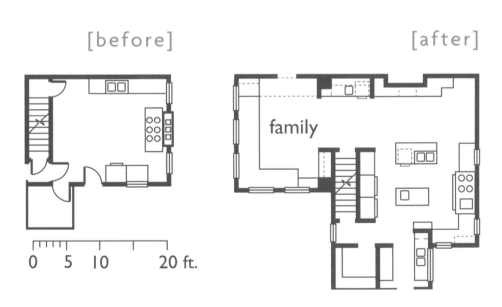

family

0   5   10   20 ft.

▲ The kitchen in this 80-year-old home was tucked into the back of the house, virtually out of sight. To create a more open, expansive layout, designers recommended tearing down the walls that originally divided the space into a warren of smaller rooms.

▲ To celebrate this home's history, the designer took cabinet doors rescued from the original butler's pantry and incorporated them into the cabinet design.

architects

Whether you're planning a large kitchen addition or simply want to bump out to increase space, consider hiring an architect. Experts in structural, electrical and plumbing systems, architects are also artists who can bring beauty to every aspect of a space. Architects work with the entire scope of a project, from designing a space to ensuring that it is structurally sound to specifying materials and products. Architects are also knowledgeable about building codes and zoning laws.

Your initial meeting with an architect can take place in your home. Discuss your general ideas for the project—how much more space you need, what look you're going for—and then ask the architect to explain the firm's design philosophy and specializations. Show the architect photos of kitchens you admire. The architect, in turn, will show you a portfolio of work the firm has completed.

During the meeting, look for a common viewpoint and a rapport. Inquire

EXPERT TIPS

Set Ground Rules

Once you've decided on a project timetable, put the terms of your agreement in writing. Make sure your architect is willing to embark on a partnership in which communication lines are open for brainstorming and turning dreams into plans on paper.

about experience and disclose your budget. Find out what the architect will charge to oversee construction and how many site visits this generally entails. Charges might consist of a percentage of construction costs (five to 15 percent is common), a set fee, hourly rates, a sum per square foot built or a combination of these methods. Extra planning sessions may be billed hourly. Before committing to an architect, visit a couple of completed houses the firm has worked on and check references.

Generally, your architect will work with you to plan the new space, submitting several sets of drawings for your approval. This concludes with a final set of construction plans that gives the contractor detailed specifications—from the kitchen's dimensions to product placement.

▲ Architects designed a gracious barrel-vaulted ceiling over the bar to lend the space a sense of drama and set it off from rooms on either side.

▲ An architect designed this thick, brick arched hallway leading to a library, echoing the home's European character.

▲ A good architect will consider everything, from improving traffic flow to increasing the amount of natural light in your kitchen. The French doors that were added to this dining area solve both challenges.

contractors

The general contractor (GC) is the person who takes architectural plans and brings them to life. When screening for potential candidates, look for a contractor who possesses experience in the field, proven results, strong leadership abilities and excellent communication skills. Before choosing a contractor, schedule interviews with at least three candidates. Once you've found the best, it takes work on your part to keep your relationship productive and positive.

Like your architect, the contractor should be familiar with local building codes. The GC should also procure all necessary building permits—a responsibility that should be specified in your contract. Contractors will hire and supervise the trades people, called subcontractors or "subs," involved in the project (including tile setters, electricians and plumbers) and coordinate work schedules and procedures.

Contractors' fees come in three different forms; make sure you know how the contractor charges before accepting a bid. Some contractors work on a "cost-plus" basis, charging a fee for services plus the cost of the project (materials, services of subcontractors, etc.). Others have a fixed fee—the best option, since you know ahead of time what to expect. Still others work on a percentage of the total cost. If your contractor works on percentage, make sure you keep track of expenses throughout the project and ask for a cost breakdown.

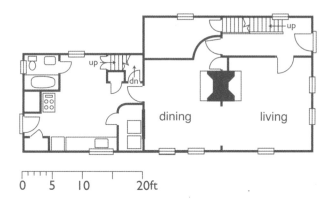

[before]

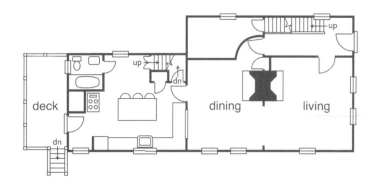

[after]

0   5   10   20ft

▲ Innovative plans from seasoned experts, such as this architect's renderings, show how much found space can be added, even within an existing footprint.

▲ The contractor on this kitchen found a way to open up a smallish kitchen. The pass-through to the living room was designed as a glass storage rack; open-ended slots make it possible to access the glasses from either room.

EXPERT TIPS

Be Thorough

When meeting prospective candidates, provide each person with the same information, so you can make an apples-to-apples comparison. Supply candidates with a written description of the work to be done, along with a materials wish list. Be clear and firm about budget and schedule requirements. Talk in detail about the contractor's past projects and ask to visit a project in progress. Follow up by calling all references and stopping by work sites.

The cost of your kitchen project is largely determined by the bids provided by professionals involved in the project. Each interested candidate should produce a written bid, complete with prices for materials and any additional service charges. Consider each bid carefully, noting what is included and what is considered "extra"—such as cleanup or debris removal. Take such fees into account when comparing higher and lower bids. And don't necessarily jump at the lowest bid: This contractor, eager for work, may have underestimated prices or scheduling. Often, the middle bid is the best one— realistic, but not inflated.

When making a final choice, pay attention to gut instincts, too. You'll be working with this professional for several weeks or months depending on the size of your kitchen renovation. He or she will be in and out of your home each day, so it's essential that you like and feel comfortable talking to the candidate you eventually hire. Before offering the job to anyone, call your local Better Business Bureau to see if any complaints have been lodged against the contractor and check to make sure he or she holds all necessary permits and insurance.

Once your project has begun, communication is the key to an effective homeowner-contractor relationship. Before work commences, make sure you've established a firm budget and schedule. The contractor should also provide you with a day-to-day outline of work to be performed. He or she should explain who each subcontractor will be, so you know who will be working in your home.

As construction progresses, hold regular meetings—either in person or by phone—to monitor progress and quality. Try not to make changes once the work has begun, but do address any concerns as soon as they arise; the longer you wait, the more expensive changes may become.

◀ To add visual interest to a line of cabinets, the contractor mixed two finishes—an especially good trick in a large space.

10 Questions to Ask Your Contractor

1. What's your specialty: low-, mid- or high-priced projects?
2. What was your last project?
3. May I have your bank references? If the contractor is in good financial standing, this request shouldn't be a problem.
4. Do you warranty your work? Many contractors offer a one-year warranty.
5. What's your fee schedule? Some contractors work for a percentage of a job's total cost, some for a flat fee and others on a "cost-plus" basis—the project's cost (materials, services, subcontractors), plus a fee.
6. How long will the work take?
7. Who will supervise the crew on-site every day?
8. Where will materials be stored?
9. What hours will you work?
10. Will I be charged for changes (other than costs for new materials) once construction has begun?

▲ The contractor on this job added many details, like custom moldings on cabinets and ceiling, to bring a one-of-a-kind look to this kitchen.

▶ Be sure to interview your contractor in person and go over the bid and contract carefully. The contractor will be the person in charge of your whole project—including any unforeseen snafus—so it is important that you have faith in his or her abilities and feel comfortable communicating any concerns.

Hiring the best professionals for your job is one way to ensure its success. One important part of comparing different contractors, architects and designers is evaluating the proposals they offer for the project. Once you've determined the professionals you'd like to have bid on your project, you'll need to write a bid request. For the bids to be accurate and comparable, you must provide identical information to each bidder, in as much detail as possible. Include plans and a list of all materials, appliances and fixtures, complete with brand names, model numbers and colors. Set a deadline for bids to be returned to you—one to three weeks is reasonable.

Once you receive bids, they should be professionally presented, typewritten on company letterhead and signed by the professional. Each one should include the following:

• A price for materials and labor. Labor must be included in the bid, otherwise you may find yourself paying much more than you might expect. Beware of a "time-and-materials" arrangement; these deals give the contractor no incentive to finish the job, exposing you to unnecessary expense.

• Fees for demolition, rebuilding, debris removal and cleaning.

• A price for all products. Double-check your materials list so nothing is overlooked.

• A statement, in writing, specifying how long the bid will be effective. If the contractor will only honor the bid for one week, you'll be out of luck if your other bids don't come in for two.

In addition, keep in mind that the cost of obtaining all necessary permits, inspections, licenses and insurance is the contractor's responsibility, and the bid should say so. The bid should also state any work that will not be completed by the contractor, such as disposing of appliances. It's often a wise idea to ask your architect or designer to look over each bid.

If you've provided all the contractors with an identical bid request, the proposed fees should not vary more than 5 to 10 percent. Be wary of any bid that comes in exceptionally low or high, and ask to meet with the contractor to go over the proposal together. For low bids, make sure the contractor has included every cost related to the job.

If a first-rate contractor submits an exceptionally high bid, ask him or her to justify the price. It may be due to scheduling conflicts or to a feature you'd be happy to do without. Keep in mind that price isn't everything. Personality, references, reputation, quality of work and schedule are key to a good collaboration, so be sure to take these factors into account during the bidding process.

▲ A project like this pantry, featuring maple panels and cherry insets, will raise costs.

Solving Problems

Though most professionals provide their own standard contracts, it is up to you to make sure that it includes appropriate provisions for your specific project. Head off potential headaches early by including:
• A plan for how each party will handle problems that arise during the project. This is usually covered with an addendum to the contract that covers any additional payments required from the homeowner to remedy the situation.
• A dispute-resolution clause. To avoid litigation, many contractors call for mediation by a third party or arbitration by a panel if a dispute cannot be settled.
• Details of the conditions under which either party can legally terminate the contract.

▲ A good designer is a worthwhile investment and can help you create a unique, highly personalized space. Adding antique twig stools complements the wood counter, while the gleam of a copper backsplash and stainless-steel hood add a lot of pizzazz.

◀ The owner of this kitchen opted to dedicate a good portion of her budget to the countertops. Stone is expensive, but it's hard to beat its beauty and durability.

budgeting & finance

▲ Rather than buying numerous high-end appliances, select a special splurge piece, such as this dual-fuel range updated with all the modern conveniences.

Nothing makes the dream of a kitchen renovation seem more real than when it comes time to consider cost. Planning a budget and procuring financing are two very important steps in the process. When compared to the excitement of choosing cabinets or tweaking layouts, crunching numbers may pale in comparison, but creating a budget and lining up funds will give you a true idea of what kind of kitchen you'll be able to create.

Since kitchen renovations invariably cost more than initial expectations, budgeting enough funds for the job is crucial. One way to start is by getting some rough estimates for design and construction fees. You can do this by setting up an in-home consultation with a certified kitchen planner. By considering the kitchen space and the kind of materials you are interested in using, as well as any plumbing or electrical issues that might crop up, an expert can usually arrive at a ballpark figure. Beyond that figure, it makes sense to add about 20 percent for a contingency "slush fund."

When formulating your budget, be sure to factor in your motivation and ultimate goal. For instance, are you fulfilling a long-time dream of creating a gourmet kitchen or merely trying to increase the resale value of your home? Determining the scope of the project, as well as the purpose of the remodeling, can guide you in developing a budget for the job. If you plan to live in the house for some time, or if you're building a new home, you may decide to go all out—the years you'll spend enjoying the new kitchen will justify the expense of including the high-end features you really want. If you are remodeling for resale, beware not to over-improve. Instead, get a sense of what other homes in your area feature to avoid investing more than the market will bear. Instead, limit improvements to visible changes that will help your house "show" well—like new flooring or countertops.

Depending on where the estimate comes in, you may need to trim or slash items to come up with a projected budget you can afford. Consider the full extent of the project, from start to finish, when creating a budget. Small finishing touches (such as wallpaper, lighting fixtures, etc.) add up and must be factored into the final cost. As you choose professionals for the job, make sure they understand and respect your budget. It will be their job to make the most of every penny.

▼ A modest kitchen still offers charm and convenience. Glass doors add a touch of elegance to stock cabinets and a butcher-block top adds a workman-like appeal to the island.

▲ An inexpensive way to bring style to a kitchen is through the use of accessories, such as these rooster canisters, which evoke a French country feel.

▲ One way to cut costs is with fool-the-eye vinyl tiles. They mimic the appearance of ceramic at a more affordable price.

▲ Can't afford a mosaic backsplash? Make a bold impact using a few eye-catching decorative tiles—like these stone inlay squares with classic French motifs—mixed with less expensive tile.

▲ Open shelves—simple and inexpensive—are a terrific option to cut costs on cabinetry and give a small kitchen a more open feel.

▲ Hunter green laminate counters—a practical and economical choice—allowed the owners of this kitchen to splurge on other materials, like their triple-bowl sink and appliances.

▲ For an interesting and less expensive alternative to additional cabinets, a free-standing buffet provides both storage and display space.

There is a wide range of financing options that you can use to pay for your kitchen renovation. To figure out which one is right for you, first determine whether you want to borrow the money for the project or fund it from your own assets. If you opt to pay from your own pocket—perhaps from a savings account or the profit on a house sale—you'll have a firm sense of what you can afford, and you'll avoid the interest charges and paperwork involved with a loan.

The more expensive your prospective project, the more likely it is that you'll want to approach a lender for at least some of the funds. Refinancing is becoming a common method for financing kitchen renovations. As home values have increased significantly in the past 10 years, many people use refinancing as a way of tapping into the equity they have accrued, both through rising values and by paying down their mortgages. During a refinance, the new mortgage amount can be greater than the outstanding mortgage balance, and the extra cash can go toward improvements.

The three main advantages of taking out a new mortgage to pay for your project are that interest rates can be fixed or locked in for the duration of the loan, the loan can be stretched over as many as 30 years so that monthly payments are lower and the interest is tax-deductible. Even if you are not ready to start your home-improvement project immediately, you can still refinance when mortgage rates are attractive and set aside the additional cash you take away from the loan in a special account to be used when the project finally gets under way.

Another way to tap into your home's equity is through a home-equity loan or a line of credit. A home-equity loan is for a lump-sum amount, whereas a line of credit allows you to draw money and repay it as you need to, up to the maximum amount approved. The maximum amount is usually up to 70 to 80 percent of the value of the house, minus the amount owed on the current mortgage.

The rates for these types of loans are usually variable, some 1 to 2.5 points above the prime rate, U.S. Treasury Bill rate or whatever index a lender ties it to. This interest is usually tax-deductible, as well. But the rate will fluctuate with the index, so it has the potential of increasing regularly and significantly over the life of the loan. The type of loan you choose will also depend on the term you prefer—or need. Mortgages usually offer a longer payback period—and therefore lower payments—than an equity loan or line of credit.

A formal, long-term loan is not the only way to finance your home-improvement project. Some contractors and larger building and remodeling firms have financing programs for customers. If you lack home equity or prefer a quick loan for a small project, a personal loan might be the answer. These loans are unsecured, so they usu-ally come with higher interest rates and a short repayment period. If you are looking at a modest loan for a short duration, you might consider putting the home-improvement costs on your credit card, but only if it is a card that offers an extremely low or zero-percent interest rate for a set amount of time. Large home-improvement retailers also offer financing programs you might want to consider. If the company you work for offers a profit-sharing or 401k program, you may be able to borrow against the money you have put aside. Regardless of which loan you choose, be sure to inquire about any application and closing costs, penalties, and interest deductibility.

▲ In this kitchen, plain, basic cabinetry is enlivened by a fun color and funky, retro hardware. Subway tiles are a simple design element that add a lot of panache.

▲ Stencils are an affordable and personalized way to enliven a kitchen space.

photography credits

Page i Peter Loppacher; **ii** Ivy D. Moriber; **iv & 5** Melabee M. Miller; **6 - 7** Langdon Clay; **7** *(right)* Courtesy of Maytag; **8** Mark Samu; **10** Mark Samu; **11** Courtesy of Amera; **12** Robert Lautman; **13** *(top)* Sam Gray, *(bottom right)* Courtesy of Kraftmaid Cabinetry, *(bottom left)* John Bessler; **14** Melabee M. Miller; **15** Drawings by Paul Mirto; **16** *(top left)* Mark Samu, *(bottom right)* Sam Gray, *(bottom left)* Lydia Gould Bessler; **17** *(top)* Bill Geddes, *(bottom right)* Sam Gray, *(bottom left)* Mark Samu; **18** Courtesy of Benjamin Moore & Company; **19** *(top)* Jason McConathy, *(bottom)* Courtesy of KitchenAid Home Appliances; **20** Jason McConathy; **21** *(top)* James F. Wilson, *(bottom right)* Courtesy of John Boos & Co., *(bottom left)* Sam Gray; **22** Courtesy of Kraftmaid Cabinetry; **23** *(top)* Courtesy of KitchenAid Home Appliances, *(bottom right)* Courtesy of LG Electronics, *(bottom left)* Courtesy of Kenmore; **24** Jason McConathy; **25** *(top, bottom right and bottom left)* Courtesy of Kraftmaid Cabinetry, *(bottom center)* Mark Samu; **26** Courtesy of Aristokraft Cabinetry; **27** *(all)* Courtesy of Kraftmaid Cabinetry; **28** *(top left, bottom right and bottom center)* Courtesy of Kraftmaid Cabinetry, *(bottom left)* Courtesy of AARP; **29** Courtesy of Kraftmaid Cabinetry; **30** Melabee M. Miller; **31** Tony Giammarino; **32** Sam Gray; **33** Sam Gray; **34** Melabee M. Miller; **35** Melabee M. Miller; **36** *(both)* Melabee M. Miller; **37** *(all)* Melabee M. Miller; **38** *(both)* Peter Loppacher; **39** *(all)* Peter Loppacher; **40** *(both)* Tony Giammarino; **41** *(all)* Tony Giammarino; **42** Ivy D. Moriber; **43** Ivy D. Moriber; **44** Ivy D. Moriber; **45** *(both)* Ivy D. Moriber; **46** *(both)* Ken Gutmaker; **47** Ken Gutmaker; **48** Mark Samu; **49** Mark Samu; **50** Mark Samu; **51** *(all)* Mark Samu; **52** Peter Loppacher; **53** *(both)* Peter Loppacher; **54** Alex Hayden; **55** *(all)* Alex Hayden; **56** Melabee M. Miller; **57** Melabee M. Miller; **58** *(both)* Melabee M. Miller; **59** Melabee M. Miller; **60** John Bessler; **61** *(both)* John Bessler; **62** Peter Loppacher; **63** *(all)* Peter Loppacher; **64** *(both)* Mark Samu; **65** *(top)* Mark Samu, *(bottom and left)* Jason McConathy; **66** *(both)* Julie Semel; **67** *(all)* Julie Semel; **68** *(top)* Mark Samu, *(bottom right)* Julie Semel; **69** *(both)* Mark Samu; **70** Mark Samu; **71** *(all)* Mark Samu; **72** *(both)* Tony Giammarino; **73** Tony Giammarino; **74** *(both)* Robert Lautman; **75** Robert Lautman; **76** *(both)* Peter Loppacher; **77** Peter Loppacher; **78** Mark Samu; **79** Mark Samu; **80** *(both)* Melabee M. Miller; **81** *(top and bottom)* Fred Housel, *(left)* Melabee M. Miller; **82** *(both)* Tony Giammarino; **83** Tony Giammarino; **84** Mark Samu; **85** Mark Samu; **86** Sam Gray; **87** *(both)* Sam Gray; **88** Jason McConathy; **89** Jason McConathy; **90** *(both)* Tony Giammarino; **91** Tony Giammarino; **92** Tony Giammarino; **93** Tony Giammarino; **94** *(both)* Mark Samu; **95** Mark Samu; **96** *(both)* Jessie Walker; **97** *(all)* Jessie Walker; **98** *(both)* Sam Gray; **99** *(all)* Sam Gray; **100** Mark Samu; **102** Courtesy of IKEA; **103** Courtesy of Aristokraft Cabinetry; **104** Courtesy of Crystal Cabinet Works; **105** *(top left)* Courtesy of Quality Custom Cabinetry, *(top right)* Courtesy of Siematic, *(bottom right)* Fred Housel; **106** *(left)* Courtesy of Plain & Fancy, *(right)* Courtesy of Merillat; **107** *(top left)* Courtesy of Kraftmaid Cabinetry, *(top right)* Courtesy of Wellborn Cabinet, Inc., *(bottom right)* Courtesy of Decora; **108** *(top right)* Courtesy of KitchenAid Home Appliances, *(bottom)* Fred Housel; **109** *(top)* Mark Samu; *(bottom)* Courtesy of Studiobecker; **110** *(left)* Courtesy of Wood-Mode Fine Custom Cabinetry, *(right)* Courtesy of Timberlake Cabinet Company; **111** *(Clockwise from upper left)* Courtesy of Restoration Hardware, Courtesy of Atlas Homewares, Courtesy of Rocky Mountain Hardware, Courtesy of Anthropologie, Courtesy of Baldwin Brass Hardware, Courtesy of Lenape, Courtesy of Target, Courtesy of Lenape, Courtesy of Kraftmaid Cabinetry; **112** Courtesy of Silestone; **113** Courtesy of Amtico; **114** *(top left)* Courtesy of IKEA, *(top right)* Courtesy of John Boos & Co.; **115** *(top right)* Courtesy of Vermont Structural Slate, *(bottom right)* Courtesy of DuPont, *(bottom left)* Courtesy of Vermont Soapstone; **116** *(left)* Courtesy of Cosentino USA, *(right)* Courtesy of Silestone; **117** *(top and left)* Courtesy of Buddy Rhodes Studio, *(bottom)* Courtesy of Ann Sacks Tile & Stone; **118** *(top left)* Courtesy of DuPont Corian, *(bottom right)* Courtesy of DuPont, *(bottom left)* Courtesy of Wilsonart; **119** *(top)* Courtesy of Avonite Surfaces, *(bottom)* Courtesy of The Craft-Art Company, *(left)* Courtesy of Samsung; **120** *(left)* Courtesy of Bruce Hardwood Floors, *(right)* Courtesy of Harmony Grow Hardwood; **121** *(top)* Courtesy of Dal-Tile, *(bottom)* Courtesy of Laufen, *(left)* Courtesy of Bruce Hardwood Floors; **122** Courtesy of Wilsonart Flooring; **123** *(top)* Courtesy of Armstrong, *(bottom and left)* Courtesy of Congoleum; **124** Courtesy of Forbo Linoleum; **125** *(top)* Courtesy of Armstrong, *(bottom)* Courtesy of Buddy Rhodes Studio; **126** *(both)* Courtesy of Imperial; **127** *(top)* Courtesy of Benjamin Moore & Company, *(bottom)* Courtesy of Walker & Zanger, *(left)* Courtesy of Thibaut, Inc.; **128** Mark Samu; **129** *(top)* Courtesy of Euro-Tile, *(bottom)* Courtesy of American Florim, *(left)* Courtesy of Walker & Zanger; **130** Courtesy of Wolf; **131** Courtesy of Maytag; **132** *(left)* Courtesy of Viking, *(right)* Courtesy of Thermador; **133** *(top)* Courtesy of Broan, *(bottom right)* Courtesy of Kenmore, *(bottom left)* Courtesy of Fisher & Paykel; **134** *(left)* Courtesy of Wolf, *(right)* Courtesy of Dacor; **135** *(top left)* Courtesy of Thermador, *(top right)* Courtesy of General Electric Company, *(bottom)* Melabee M. Miller; **136** *(left)* Courtesy of Broan, *(right)* Courtesy of Zephyr; **137** *(top)* Courtesy of Viking, *(bottom right)* Courtesy of Jenn-Air, *(bottom left)* Courtesy of Vent-A-Hood; **138** *(left)* Courtesy of Dacor, *(right)* Courtesy of Wolf; **139** *(top left)* Courtesy of Kenmore, *(top right)* Courtesy of Sharp, *(bottom)* Courtesy of General Electric Company; **140** *(left)* Courtesy of Viking, *(right)* Courtesy of Amana; **141** *(top)* Courtesy of Kenmore, *(bottom right)* Courtesy of General Electric Company, *(bottom left)* Courtesy of KitchenAid Home Appliances; **142** *(top)* Courtesy of Elmira Stove Works, *(bottom right)* Courtesy of General Electric Company, *(bottom left)* Courtesy of Viking; **143** *(top left)* Courtesy of Maytag, *(top right)* Mark Samu, *(bottom)* Courtesy of Sub-Zero; **144** *(left)* Courtesy of Fisher & Paykel, *(right)* Bill Geddes; **145** *(top left)* Courtesy of Fisher & Paykel/Bill Geddes, *(top right)* Courtesy of Maytag, *(bottom)* Courtesy of KitchenAid Home Appliances/Bill Geddes; **146** Mark Samu; **147** Courtesy of Moen, Incorporated; **148** Langdon Clay; **149** *(top)* Langdon Clay, *(bottom)* Courtesy of Jacuzzi; **150** Mark Samu; **151** *(top)* Courtesy of Price Pfister, *(bottom)* Courtesy of American Standard; **152** *(top)* Courtesy of Rohl, *(bottom)* Courtesy of Kohler Co.; **153** *(top)* Courtesy of Toto, *(bottom)* Peter Loppacher, *(left)* Melabee M. Miller; **154** *(top)* Courtesy of Grohe, *(bottom right)* Courtesy of Kallista; **155** *(top)* Mark Samu, *(bottom)* Courtesy of Sterling, *(left)* Courtesy of Delta Faucet Company; **156** Courtesy of Rico Espinet Lighting; **157** Courtesy of Milgard Windows; **158** *(both)* Courtesy of Restoration Hardware; **159** *(top left)* Courtesy of Restoration Hardware, *(top right and bottom)* Courtesy of Progress Lighting; **160** *(left)* Courtesy of Weather Shield Windows and Doors, *(right)* Courtesy of Pella Windows and Doors; **161** *(top left)* Courtesy of Vetter Windows & Doors, *(top right and bottom right)* Courtesy of Pozzi Custom Collection, *(bottom left)* Courtesy of Marvin Windows and Doors; **162** Courtesy of Peachtree Doors and Windows; **163** *(top)* Courtesy of Marvin Windows and Doors, *(bottom right and bottom left)* Courtesy of Andersen Windows and Doors; **164** *(top)* Courtesy of Hurd Windows, *(bottom right)* Courtesy of Pella Windows and Doors, *(bottom left)* Courtesy of Eagle Window & Door, Inc.; **165** *(top left and bottom)* Courtesy of Caradco, *(top right)* Courtesy of Weather Shield Windows and Doors; **166** Langdon Clay; **168** Jessie Walker; **170** Jessie Walker; **171** *(top)* Jessie Walker, *(left)* Drawing by John Kocon, *(bottom)* Mark Samu; **172** Langdon Clay; **173** *(top and bottom right)* Langdon Clay, *(bottom center and bottom left)* Drawings by Mirto Art Studio; **174** Langdon Clay; **175** *(top)* Langdon Clay, *(bottom right and bottom left)* Jessie Walker; **176** Mark Samu; **177** *(top left and top right)* Drawings by John Kocon, *(bottom)* Mark Samu; **178** Courtesy of Fieldstone Cabinetry; **179** *(top)* Courtesy of Wood-Mode Fine Custom Cabinetry, *(bottom)* Corbis; **180** Sam Gray; **181** *(top)* Melabee M. Miller, *(bottom)* Sam Gray; **182** Tim Murphy; **183** Courtesy of Elmira Stove Works; **184** Sam Gray; **185** *(top left)* Courtesy of Mariposa, *(top right)* Courtesy of Armstrong, *(bottom right)* Courtesy of Progress Lighting, *(bottom left)* Courtesy of Walker & Zanger; **186** *(left)* Doug Walker, *(right)* Courtesy of StarMark Cabinetry; **187** *(top)* Courtesy of IKEA/Bill Geddes, *(bottom)* Mark Samu.

index